TIGERS

&

ICE

Books by Edward Hoagland

Essays

The Courage of Turtles
Walking the Dead Diamond River
Red Wolves and Black Bears
The Edward Hoagland Reader
(edited by Geoffrey Wolff)
The Tugman's Passage
Heart's Desire
Balancing Acts
Tigers & Ice

Travel

Notes from the Century Before: A Journal from British Columbia
African Calliope: A Journey to the Sudan

Fiction

Cat Man
The Circle Home
The Peacock's Tail
Seven Rivers West
The Final Fate of Alligators

TIGERS

& ICE

Reflections on Nature and Life

EDWARD HOAGLAND

The Lyons Press

Printed in Canada
Design and composition by V&M Graphics, Inc.

10   9   8   7   6   5   4   3   2   1

The Library of Congress Cataloging-in-Publication Data is available on file.

Acknowledgment is given to the magazines in which these essays, sometimes under a different title, first appeared. "Behold Now Behemoth" and "Heaven and Nature" appeared in *Harper's*. "Tigers and Ice" and "Stepping Back" are from *The New York Times Magazine*. "Running Mates" was published in *Hungry Mind Review*. "A Peaceable Kingdom" appeared in *Preservation*. "Headwork" is from *Portland*. "Earth's Eye" was published in *Sierra*. "I Have Seen the Elephant" appeared in *Outside*. "Roadless Regions: A Journal Sampler" is part of the anthology *Literary Outtakes*. "Wild Things" appeared in *Granta* and *River City*.

For my mother, Helen (1902–1998);
and my daughter, Molly (married, 1998);
and for Trudy

CONTENTS

INTRODUCTION

A writer's work is to witness things. He goes to India without proffering stopgap solutions to the economic problems he sees, and to Africa without trying to fine-tune the time line of human evolution—then to Antarctica without formulating optical theories of why ice may be white, blue, or green. In the sciences, any humdrum practitioner now understands more of the sinews of physics than Isaac Newton did, whereas only a madman among writers would claim to know more about human nature than Tolstoy, Balzac, or Dickens. Genius in the arts is not eclipsed, as it is in science, because artists do not investigate fixed phenomena, but bear witness.

Most of us, however, do have an overall tale to tell; and I've been working at mine since I began my first book in 1952. These recent essays, from my early sixties, are visually emphatic because I'd just had the experience of being legally blind for a couple of years and, for the same reason, are probably love letters to life. Indeed, if "biology is chemistry with history," as somebody has said, then nature writing is biology with love. We all may love our work as a vocation, but no writer needs to be as dispassionate as a scientist is when seeking proof positive to explain an event (although the supposedly immutable Latin names that Thoreau listed in enumerating the plants and animals in his fields and woods appear to have changed more than the vernacular names he also gave).

Thoreau, in the classic way of nature writers, was a social conservative yet a political radical—disliking railroads but using the Underground Railway to spirit slaves toward freedom in Canada. There may be no escape from technology's warp, from the railroad to the Internet, but the next century's primary effort will perhaps be to reduce, ameliorate, or at least put a crimp in our current binge of innovation. Already, many people are turning back to the radio for information, in preference to the intrusions of TV, and buying four-wheel-drive vehicles, as if their suburban roads weren't paved. They complain of the airlessness of cyberspace: no moisture or fortuitous scents and random sounds; information like skim ice—so thin—or encapsulated like a sound-bite script, with "derivative" financial markets, and great music lathered on like wallpaper if you want.

John Keats toasted "confusion to mathematics" at a dinner party in 1817, having written earlier that books like Newton's *Opticks* might "unweave the rainbow." And Einstein said, in *Living Philosophies*: "Strange is our situation here upon Earth. Each of us comes for a short visit, not knowing why, yet sometimes seeming to divine a purpose. . . . The most beautiful thing we can experience is the mysterious . . . the source of all true art and science. He to whom this emotion is a stranger, who can no longer pause to wonder and stand rapt in awe, is as good as dead; his eyes are closed."

That silence and a night sky are rare commodities for most of us is the doing of engineers and other triumphalists, not him. And also ours, because of what we've shelled out money for. Common sense might have been a corrective if our consumer passions hadn't overridden our leeriness of triumphalism. Ordinary people, after all, were calling cigarettes "coffin nails" as early as 1888, according to my dictionary, about a century before the medical profession formally did. And I remember as a boy of ten discovering, like any farmer, chickens' "pecking order," maybe a decade before zoologists organized an official announcement of it—then, as a boy of nineteen, while taking care of circus elephants, sensing (no doubt like any bush hunter) their low-frequency, infrasonic method of serious communication, thirty years before scientific papers began suggesting the same.

I've traveled in Africa with professional aid-group people—better men than I—who seemed, however, able to either see the holocaust of wildlife that was under way *or* register the famine ravaging some of the tribes in areas that we were in. Possibly they could function most effectively if they were blind to one tragedy or the other, but my job as a traveling writer was to respond, in temporary terms, to both.

"I have seen the Elephant," American frontiersmen used to say, when they returned to civilization from the vast spectacles of the unknown interior. (Not—you'll notice—"I have killed the Elephant.") But children are now taught to outgrow their interest in animals by puberty and shift their outdoor attention to golf or the tennis court, where class distinctions can be applied. Yet Marxism has been just as fierce a destroyer of wild nature as capitalism, in the same way that areas of the world influenced by the Eastern religious traditions are in no better shape than Judeo-Christianity's realm. We lately think we "know" so much about nature because we have destroyed so much natural diversity, not to mention human cultures by the hundreds that were marginalized or obliterated with all their expertise and lore. By steamrollering so much of the world we have simplified it for ourselves, and therefore get the idea that we understand what's left.

The central question may soon become how much we think we want to learn about what hasn't been incinerated, lest more be monkeyed with; learning so often leads to monkeying. And the flabbergasting changes we have wrought do seem to me to be mostly monkeying—an advanced brand, featuring bulldozers, salaciousness, and lots of money. When I am exhausted or disheartened, I sometimes play circus music, from Merle Evans and his Ringling Bros. band. Though these selections are often by John Philip Sousa, a Marine Corps bandmaster, they don't sound military—no longer music to kill or die by. When played with lilt and syncopation, they become poignant and chameleon—music by which to dance on a high wire or improvise a clown act or play with a tiger and survive, even thrive. When negotiating with the force of gravity, or with a pride of lions, you foil, not crush, the lions' charge, so you will have their partnership tomorrow, and make light of gravity's pull, instead of treating it like machine-gun fire. Limber hands, not marching feet, because gravity will also be around tomorrow.

What I'm suggesting is that if we can turn technology around, like the reading of a tune, to a different sort of emphasis, we can reverse the momentum of worldwide destruction and monitor, then parry the cascade of pollution, promoting habitat reclamation and the survival, too, of tottering human cultures. It would require a change of spirit as well as rejiggering the thrust of the technological instrumentation we use—the clarinets to lilt a bit and toodle, the slide trombones to oompah, the trumpets to gild the lily, when not twitching their sharp shoulders, the drums to pile on unexpectedly, then dare to skip a beat or so.

When peasants wipe out a rain forest to grow subsistence food, it's one thing, but corporations chewing up the oxygen-producing integument of the world for a better profit margin is quite another. They ought to be taxed heavily by the United Nations. Though the urgencies are manifold, I hate the canary-in-the-coal-mine argument that conservationists are forced to use—for example, that if populations of frogs all over are being deformed by acid rain or are dying out because increasing ultraviolet radiation injures their eggs, *we* should worry because it might portend analogous damage to *us*. What's in store for us may indeed be unnerving and ultimately unstring our genes. But I care wholeheartedly also about what's happening to the frogs.

Even on my own patch of land in Vermont, which I like to think of as a sanctuary, I noticed a pickerel frog last summer with a withered hind leg. Investigators are finding that 8 percent of their samplings in the state are visibly deformed, versus a normal average of about 1 percent. But mine alone was one too many. The first vertebrate music on land was probably frogs', and if you think about it, the first humanoid shape may have been some form of paleontological frog. Mammals that once were day dwellers, as frontier diaries attest, have become nocturnal in order to coexist with us, and many species of birds are improvising fragmentary homes in shattered habitats. But since amphibians can't run or fly, they're stuck in front of the earthmovers, and even in a refuge are calamitously thin-skinned under a corrosive sun. I feel for them.

These essays were informed by that spell of semiblindness I'd had, which, like turning sixty, did tend to focus my priorities. Though I've published five books of fiction too, essays became my special genre about thirty years ago because I seemed best suited to doing them: a bad stutter from childhood made me want to "talk." One sails a bit against the wind, however, to work for three decades as an essayist. Essays sell more easily than fiction to magazines and win a quicker audience, but are a kind of literary stepchild because a taint of glibness attaches to the form—from countless op-ed columns, style-page plaints, radio guest-piece pontifications, and observations tossed off almost as casually as telling everybody last night's dream. Real essays come harder than that, but the word somehow sounds fustian (an astronaut recently asked me what an "essay" is), despite the transformation to a more demotic mode. Yet wrestling with them can be an adventure; and because they are intended to be reflective, one may age into them quite well. Though a Luddite about computers, I believe, too, that the essay's resilience, already four hundred years old, will weather on and maybe profit from the World Wide Web.

TIGERS
& ICE

BEHOLD NOW
BEHEMOTH

A bristly, lovely, although hot and fearsome recklessness invigorates God in the Old Testament when he loses patience. *Behold now behemoth, which I made with thee,* he says to Job, who has been complaining of his unjust sufferings. But justice is not what the majesty of Creation is all about. Consider, for instance, the hippopotamus. *He moveth his tail like a cedar . . . his bones are like bars of iron . . .*

For me too religion needs to wear a mask of jubilation. Yet unmixed glee is beyond my capacities. I begin to flag if I am required to be upbeat for many hours at a stretch— though I have in fact had just the sort of biblical experience that warrants a lifelong commitment to the happy tangents of faith. It happened during my late fifties, when two eye operations restored my sight after three years of legal blindness. My vision had shrunk to the point where I couldn't see faces, birds, or trees. Through my telescope I studied the rising moon or the way that branches interlaced, but even the lenses of such an instrument could barely recapitulate what my eyes with ordinary eyeglasses had formerly seen.

Quite suddenly, however, within a period of half a dozen weeks, the miracle of the streaming clouds, the blowing grass, the leaping birds, the upspread trees, and the variety of expressions on my friends' faces was given back to me. For possibly an entire year, in the exalting aftermath of regaining my eyesight, I was incapable of being depressed. I simply needed to glance out the window and couldn't believe how golden the sunshine was, how softly green each leaf, or how radiant the city night could be, with its great arclike sparkling bridges and hooded mobs of apartment houses, each of the thousands of lives packed inside signified by a small yellow light. If I was in the city, the slant of lion-skinned building stone on a skyscraper's face was breathtaking. In the country, I was lifted to rapture by the prismatic pointillism of the wildflowers, or a sea of seed heads shimmering underneath the black outcrops on a mountainside, the puce and pink of a slow dawn, the white slats of birch bark under a purple rainstorm medallioned by a rainbow or slashed by a crimson shaft of half-set sun, a sky big enough to fall right into forever and ever if I lay on my back and didn't grip the grass.

And, of course, I didn't neglect to look up Christ's miracle-working episodes, impromptu as they were. Set against the scale of eternal redemption, the temporary plight of the blind and sick whom he had encountered accidentally was not his preoccupation. But pity for their anguish mixed with his practicality when he asked whether they "believed." Presumably, since God had created heaven and earth, God could cure blindness, leprosy, or whatnot with or without "belief," but Christ's own powers, swift and serene though they seem, may have needed that extra catalyst. Indeed, in Mark 8, the act requires two applications of Christ's hands:

the first restores the blind man of Bethsaida's sight only to the extent that people look to him *like trees . . . walking about.* So *Jesus laid his hands on his eyes again.* Rather like my surgeon.

I was truly, sadly startled, though, in the midst of my exuberance, to notice how many of my friends' faces had changed during my blind years. They looked battered, bruised, disheartened, bereft of illusion, apprehensive, or knocked a bit awry by the very campaigns and thickets of life that I was giddy with delight to have regained. I was seeing the forest, I decided, while they were engrossed by the trees. Like a prisoner sprung from a dungeon, I didn't care about minor harassments, frictions, frettings, inconveniences. The sky, the clouds, the colors and movement, and my sudden freedom were plenty for me. I could be irascible, impatient, and hard to get on with, but never unhappy; that's not what life was for. Instead I was charged up, alight, Lazarus-like, and I realized that such a marked alteration in my friends' faces and the cast of strangers' expressions could not be the result of my having just been "away" for a while, but that everything was clearer. The fox-red coat of a deer in June; the glow of a checkered, fat garter snake, its white skin shining between its black scales; a goldfinch's trampoline bounce on the wing; the fire-engine pace of a chimney swift tearing around; leaf shadows running on a tree trunk like a crowd of squirrels as the wind blew. Such a lovely, vivid, vibrant world—what does it matter if your marriage is going rancid? "Cheer up, for heaven's sake!" I wanted to say when the shaft of a stranger's glance on the street told me a tale of misery. Funky neon at midnight in the city, or raindrops zigging down a windowpane, a sky of feather-blue, a sky of sleety pewter, a lady's dachshund walking like a leashed salamander down the sidewalk (and the piercing pleasure of a toddler seeing it), old bricks on a town house or a church front.

In Manhattan I went to services at the church where I'd been christened more than fifty years before, and both before and after my crucial operations I seemed so otherworldly or beamish to the vicars and the vergers that they assumed I was one of the homeless, fiftyish men who were mingling with the well-heeled parishioners for the sake of the sandwiches served afterward. There was no end to how glad I was at any hour to wake up, step outside, or simply pour and stir a cup of coffee and stretch my feet into the spill of zebra-patterned sunlight that the venetian slats threw on the rug so marvelously.

Behold now behemoth, God says. . . . *He lieth under the shady trees, in the covert of the reed . . . the willows of the brook compass him about. Behold, he drinketh up a river, and hasteth not: he trusteth that he can draw up Jordan into his mouth.* Or, God continues angrily to Job, *Canst thou draw out leviathan with an hook. . . . Canst thou put an hook into his nose? . . . Will he make many supplications unto thee? . . . Wilt thou play with him as with a bird?*

I use the King James translation, and Leviathan may be either a whale or a crocodile, though this spiky, vivid description goes on to resemble in its particulars a scaly, toothy crocodile, who, like the often dangerous hippo, could make the Jordan River terrifying. The biblical Hebrews were an inland people, not seafarers like the Phoenicians; but on the other hand, the author of the Book of Job is considered to have been a later, more traveled and worldly individual than some of the other writers. The Revised English Bible of 1989 splits this chapter, 41, into two entries divided by Chapter 40, so that Leviathan can represent both of these wondrous and unconquerable creatures. And the whole glorious dithyramb to the animal kingdom—peacocks, lions, wild gleeful goats, formidable wild oxen, wild nifty asses, dashing ostriches, soaring cliff eagles—recited by God pridefully to the much abused Job out of a "whirlwind," is in marked contrast to that earlier, more famous God, whose injunction to Adam and Eve at the beginning of Genesis is that they and humankind should *subdue . . . and have dominion over the fish of the sea, and over the fowl of the air, and over every living thing that moveth upon the earth.*

The Hebrew God is whimsical, jealous, inconsistent: mad, of course, very soon after that first chapter of Genesis, at Eve and Adam, with somewhat the same tone of thunderous petulance he later directs at poor Job for rather less reason. (Job's long sufferings have been the result of a sort of a sporting bet between God and a manipulative, teasing Satan, not punishment for an impulsive act of disobedience at the behest of some newly fledged Serpent.) Even in the single book of Deuteronomy, where Moses transmits, at God's instruction in Chapter 5, the Ten Commandments (plus at different points a considerable amount of merciful detail as to how bond servants, widows, orphans, and destitute wayfarers shall be treated), God also decrees, in Chapters 2 and 3, the genocide of the tribes of Heshbon—*the men, and the women, and the little ones*—and also of Og—*utterly destroying the men, women, and children, of every city.* And again, in Chapter 20, God ordains a further holocaust: *Thou shalt save alive nothing that breatheth. But thou shalt utterly destroy them; namely, the Hittites, and the Amorites, the Canaanites, and the Perizzites, the Hivites, and the Jebusites; as the Lord thy God hath commanded thee.* Deuteronomy does contain the brief, winsomely generous admonition in Chapter 25 that *thou shalt not muzzle the ox when he treadeth out the corn* (in other words, not let him feel hunger), but it also includes, in Chapter 28, the dire warning that if God's established "holy people," the Jews, don't follow his commandments, they will become cannibals from famine, conquest, siege, and plague, eating their own children. And in Exodus 20 and 34 the vindictive threat is floated that a father's sins will be visited upon his children even to the fourth generation—although, in fairness, Deuteronomy 24, Jeremiah 30, and Ezekiel 18 contradict this. *I wound, and I heal*, he says in Deuteronomy 32.

He seems a berserk and hideous deity in some of the more perfervid remarks that Moses and others record or attribute to him. He is an angry caliph who might better suit the Serbs or Hutus of the 1990s or the Hitlerian Catholics of World War II, and he did not have much appeal for me as a boy, though the Old Testament stories we heard in church and Sunday school were riveting—the drama of baby Isaac almost being sacrificed by his father, Abraham; of Judith cutting off the head of Holofernes; of Joseph sold into slavery by his brothers; of little Moses in the bulrushes; of Job's faith and loss of faith; of David fighting Goliath with a slingshot; of Samson rendered powerless when the treacherous Delilah cut off his hair (Judith a heroine but Delilah a villainess). The sheer, gala accretion of these tales, extending over a good number of centuries, had more narrative weight than did the thirty-year story of Jesus, from Bethlehem to Calvary.

But Jesus spoke for a God whose teachings I could better swallow. His, too, in its abbreviated way, is a matchless tale. Born in a manger, although he was the Son of God, because there was no room at the inn, yet visited in his infancy by wise men and shepherds drawn by a radiant star; healing blind men and lepers, raising the dead, and throwing the money changers out of the Temple, accompanied by a small band of "fishers of men"; betrayed by Judas for thirty pieces of silver and crucified between two criminals, dying in agony and thirst after several hours but forgiving his captors, "for they know not what they do," and on the third day rising from the dead to sit at the right hand of God himself. A most direct parable—just lengthy enough, yet coherent and confirmed by four testimonials. You can't beat it for what it is, and the interpretations within our own language and time have ranged from "Onward, Christian Soldiers" to Martin Luther King. You see on TV the pomp of the Pope, versus Mother Teresa. And whatever these elaborations have become, the central addenda of Christianity seem as essential to me as the Bill of Rights added onto a basic Constitution. Judaism without the Sermon on the Mount seems a religion incomplete, *lex talionis*—an eye for an eye— without the Golden Rule: *Whatsoever ye would that men should do to you, do ye even so to them* (Matthew 7).

Jesus added to the undercarriage of Judaism not to destroy *but to fulfill*, he says. And like Moses before him, he went into the wilderness on a walkabout, up to a mountaintop for revelation—which I take to be more evidence of biblical ambivalence about the idea in Genesis that the wilderness ought to be bridled and ruled, that the snake and crocodile, the elephant and hippo, the whale and lion should have no untrammeled territory left in which to strut their stuff and play their fateful, antique roles. Still, as against the legend of Christ, shimmering and imperishable as it is (and, indeed, priests and ministers wear desert dress), you have Judaism beginning not with a baby's birth but with the very universe. You have the theater of Eve and her Serpent; then Noah's brave Ark; wise Solomon; the visions of Isaiah; Jeremiah and Zechariah; Daniel in the Lions' Den; Jonah in the Whale; the Song of Songs; and zestfully on. No wonder so many Jews have regarded themselves as a people chosen by God.

My own bias is against a monotheism so people-centered, and thus the Old Testament God who most appeals to me is least "Hebrew." ("There is no certainty that the author was an Israelite," says Marvin Pope, a leading scholar of the Book of Job.) God's magnificently hair-raising answer to Job from out of the whirlwind outguns anything of the sort in the New Testament, which after all is more fit for the advent of Saint Francis, lover of tiny birds, or the pacifism of Martin Luther King than for the preservation of old values. *Where wast thou when I laid the foundations of the earth?* God declares (a lover of carnivorous tigers as well as small birds).

> *... When the morning stars sang together? ... Hast thou commanded the morning since thy days? ... Hast thou entered into the springs of the sea? ... Have the gates of death been opened unto thee? ... Hast thou perceived the breadth of the earth? ... Where is the way where light dwelleth? and as for darkness, where is the place thereof? ... Hath the rain a father? or who hath begotten the drops of dew? Out of whose womb came the ice? and the hoary frost of heaven? ... Knowest thou the ordinances of heaven? ... Canst thou lift up thy voice to the*

*clouds? . . . Canst thou send lightnings? . . . Wilt thou
hunt the prey for the lion? or . . . provideth for the raven
his food?*

For me, that's plenty good enough as an underlying Constitution, an underpinning for my American Transcendentalism, as well as a basic link to other world religions and
beyond them to the grandfather, or "pagan," spiritual impulses that occasionally well up in so many of us at the
ocean, in the woods, or during slam-crash thunderstorms or
to the extraordinary hallucinations that afflict us when
someone we love dies. Genesis's intolerance of wilderness
was tailor-made for the Industrial Revolution. It covered the
clergy on every lame excuse they gave for ducking their
heads as the skies and fields and rivers turned sooty-black
and breathing space and sunny light and a whole panoply of
flashing creatures disappeared. Just as on other issues, such
as slavery, child labor, racial prejudice, and colonial genocide, the church was rarely in the vanguard to intervene but,
rather, brought up the rear of the mainstream, snubbing the
earnest mavericks while the situation rapidly grew worse.
In my lifetime alone, perhaps half the species that were alive
on earth when I was born will have been snuffed out.

Christianity displays these contradictions in Saint
George slaying the dragon while Saint Francis plays with
birds, in Androcles plucking a thorn from the lion's paw
while Saint Patrick drives the snakes out of Ireland. And
Judaism has faced its own immiscibility in the task of peace-
making in Israel, where rabbis and religious folk have not
seemed to play an adequate part in whatever reconciliation
has been accomplished with the Palestinians. Instead, it's
been mostly the work of military men and secular idealists,

as if the Jewish religion itself is incomplete, a religion of resistance, of "silence, exile, and cunning" (in James Joyce's analogous definition of how art should be engendered), but not yet a religion brought to closure, not yet a savior's religion here on earth.

No stretch of grief or the imagination, no precedent in science or logic can get a handle on this catastrophe—half of Creation extinguished in a single life span. Noah did not materialize again to save God's handiwork, or even a Mother Teresa. Flying beings, swimming things, creeping, crawling, running existences, long-legged or short-winged, brought to life over many, many millennia, had no escape and simply blinked out. People, says a friend of mine who is a Congregational minister, "are born in solidarity with Creation but live in brokenness with Creation," or, as he adds, "in sin."

The author of the Song of Songs, another extravaganza, might testify to that. You may recall some of his imagery: *Your eyes are doves behind your veil, your hair like a flock of goats streaming down Mount Gilead. Your teeth are like a flock of ewes newly shorn . . . your parted lips . . . like a pomegranate cut open. . . . Your two breasts like two fawns, twin fawns of a gazelle grazing among the lilies.* (This from the Revised English Bible, which is more lyric here.) *Come with me,* the speaker adds to his new bride, *from the summit of Amana, from the top of Senir and Hermon, from the lions' lairs, and the leopard-haunted hills,* to civilization. The duality of nature in the Bible is like that in other ancient epics, such as *Gilgamesh,* the *Odyssey,* or *Beowulf,* and our own literary figures, Melville, Hardy, and Conrad. Psalm 104 boasts affectionate references to wild goats and rock badgers, storks, whales that sport in the sea, wild donkeys, and young lions *seeking their food from God.*

But in Psalm 102, *I am stricken, withered like grass. . . . I am like a desert owl in the wilderness, like an owl that lives among ruins*, the writer says. Though the King James Version uses the intriguing alternative translation, "pelican of the wilderness," wild places are not habitats where you'd want to be.

And in Isaiah, Chapter 34, after the Lord has sated his bloody wrath upon the residents of Edom, *horned owl and bustard will make it their home; it will be the haunt of screech-owl and raven. . . . It will be the lair of wolves. . . . Marmots will live alongside jackals. . . . There too the night-jar will return to rest and . . . there the sand-partridge will make her nest, lay her eggs and hatch them, and gather her brood under her wings; there will the kites gather, each with its mate . . . they will occupy it for all time, and each succeeding generation will dwell there.* (The King James substitutes unicorns and cormorants, bitterns, dragons, satyrs, and vultures for some of these; and the American Revised Standard Version, porcupines, ostriches, and hyenas.) Likewise, when Babylon is overthrown in Isaiah 13, *marmots will have their lairs in her, and porcupines will overrun her houses; desert-owls will dwell there, and there he-goats will gambol; jackals will occupy her mansions, and wolves her luxurious palaces.* Sounds like the epitome of desolation but also like a bit of fun. The desert fathers lived closer to nature than we do.

Here, as in Job, the wilderness is presented as an antithesis to cities and to agriculture, certainly not one that man wishes for, yet one that, for God's superbly diverse purposes, continues to celebrate the glory of life on earth. Though God had been mean to that Snake, back in Genesis, for tempting Eve (*Upon thy belly shalt thou go, and dust shalt thou eat all the days of thy life: And I will put enmity between thee and the woman, and between thy seed and her seed . . .*), wild animals are generally God's children, too. What he envisions for them at the end of time is summed up in Isaiah 11. *Then the wolf will live with the lamb, and the leopard lie down with the kid; the calf and the young lion will feed together, with a little child to tend them. The cow and the bear will be friends . . . and the lion will eat straw like cattle. The infant will play over the cobra's hole, and the young child dance over the viper's nest. There will be neither hurt nor harm in all my holy mountain; for the land will be filled with the knowledge of the Lord as the waters cover the sea.*

No permission is given in Isaiah, Job, or Genesis for the holocaust mankind has visited upon the natural world, whereby the rhinoceros may soon be as scarce as the unicorn. Behemoths, crocodiles, and the soaring eagles and fearsome lions that enriched, mythologized, and demonized the banks of the Jordan as manifestations of God's majesty are long gone, with their like being pursued to the edge of the planet. The blackened woods, the sooty skies, Leviathan more than decimated: God is not just. He is cryptic, elliptical, even countenancing your death, *my* death. Like sand in a wasp-waisted egg timer, we tumble through the slot before we're quite ready to, and the tumbling process does not ensure fairness even in priority. You and I, born the same year, may die thirty years apart. Justice is not God's department; justice is a man-made concept, except in the somewhat different sense that character is often fate as, in fact, Job's is, finally winning him back God's favor or, to be exact, *fourteen thousand sheep, and six thousand camels, a thousand yoke of oxen, and as many she-asses,* so that he's exactly twice as rich as before God allowed Satan to toy so cruelly with him. In life we don't necessarily see people receiving their just desserts, but over a couple of decades we do notice their muddied faces and bitten nails if, although as rich as Croesus, they have lived nastily. Time wounds all heels.

The Old Testament God seemed as primitive as a tribal sheik, being too much constructed in the splintered, banal image of man. Thus the New Testament, although less dramatically embellished with centuries' worth of narrative, convinced me more as a boy. I was a Tolstoyan then, and from that teenage base of idealism I discovered jubilee "shout" singing in the black Pentecostal church I used to go to in San Francisco in the late 1950s. I later discovered Saint Francis's hymn of adoration called "The Canticle of the Creatures":

> Most high and most holy, most powerful Lord. . . .
>   To Thee and Thy creatures we proffer our praise:
> To our brother the sun in the heavens ashine,
> Who brings us the beauty and joy of our days,
> Thine emblem and sign.
> We praise thee, O Lord, for our sister the moon, . . .
> For our brother the wind, for the bright of the noon,
> For all of Thy weather.
> For our sister the water, so humble and chaste,
> For beautiful fire, with his perilous powers,
> For our mother the earth, who holds us embraced,
> Who delights us with flowers . . .

Transcendentalism naturally followed, and I stopped describing myself as a Christian. Nevertheless, Psalm 148 does say it all: *Praise the Lord from the earth, you sea monsters and ocean depths; fire and hail, snow and ice, gales of wind that obey his voice; all mountains and hills; all fruit trees and cedars; wild animals and all cattle, creeping creatures and winged birds . . . Praise the Lord.* And Psalm 150, the famous one: *Praise the Lord. Praise God in his holy place, praise him in the mighty vault of heaven. . . . Praise him with fanfares on the trumpet, praise him on harp and lyre; praise him with tambourines and dancing, praise him with flute and strings; praise him with the clash of cymbals; with triumphant cymbals praise him . . .*

Behold now behemoth, which I made with thee! An electrifying injunction, and for practically a lifetime I've been doing just that—observing zebras, and genuine behemoths like elephants, hippos, giraffes, whales, jaguars, and grizzlies. I have believed that they were indeed "made with me," and by the age of eighteen I was already thrusting my hand down a circus hippo's mouth to scratch the back of her tongue and the inside of her cheeks, much in the way that tickbirds, or "oxpeckers," do in Africa, searching out leeches. I also communed with Siberian and Sumatran tigers, both now almost extinct, and black-maned lions and Indian elephants, and I rubbed a rhino's itchy lips on sweltering afternoons, not in a trivializing manner but single-mindedly, with a passion that had begun with turtles when I was five or six—like that of city kids for dinosaurs nowadays. Leopard seals and eponymous leopards, killer whales in the Arctic and Antarctic, and Nile River crocodiles: I've traveled far and wide since then to glimpse these stirring beings. *Canst thou draw out leviathan with an hook? . . . Will he make many supplications unto thee?* Can you *make a banquet of him* or *part him among the merchants?* God asks Job jeeringly, and, alas, it's come to pass that we can, with religion frequently a handmaiden to the merchants.

On the street, with my rejuvenated sight—fifteen-thousand-dollar plastic implants—I seemed to see right back into the exhaustion and poignant anxiety in the recesses of other people's eyes, the thwarted potential for love and fun and dedication, the foiled altruism, now in abeyance, and the exasperation. And yet I could also see the imp that lived in them, the child that hadn't died. So often the variables that exist in somebody's face, from mirth to aggravation, add up to the wish to still believe in virtue, hope, and God.

"I have seen the Elephant," the Gold Rushers and other frontiersmen used to say after they returned to town. For me, with a lifelong belief that heaven is on earth, not nebulously up in the sky, I see it every dawn and sunset, and in the head-high joe-pye weed, smelling like vanilla in July (and used by the Indians in treating typhus, colds, chills, "sore womb after childbirth," diarrhea, liver and kidney ailments, "painful urination," gout, and rheumatism). I see it in the firmament at night and in a stand of spruce or a patch of moss beside a brook. And during the time when I was blind I could smell it in the scent of a blossoming basswood tree, or hear it in a toad's trill, or lay my head flat on the ground and gaze at the forest of fervent moss, inches away, a beetle or a caterpillar crawling. *Behold now behemoth.*

TIGERS AND ICE

—◆—

What do you do when you're sixty and haven't rehearsed for it? Well, to take an example, though I've cut my own hair for thirty years, this spring for the first time I put the trimmings out on the lawn for the various birds that search for hair to weave into their nests. And, using an audiotape, I've learned to identify many more bird calls than I knew at fifty, and ten times as many as when I was twenty. I'm up before six, and when the dawn's chorus ceases I play other music, knitting an aural nest of Bach for organ, Beethoven for piano, Louis Armstrong, *My Fair Lady*, Edith Piaf, *Peter Grimes*, each day's menu impromptu (my dogs bark sharply when the whale songs come on)— seldom much that I didn't listen to decades ago, but I pay more attention because after a spell of eye trouble, music and visual color seem central now.

I'm more moderate, gentler in judgment, less self-conscious, though quite cranky, yet recognizing other people's right to be cranky too. For the sake of harmony I take more for granted and skim over more. I'm still astonished, however, ineradicably so, by my generation's failure to push past token gestures to change the world for the good and to be less greedy and violence-prone than the generations before. But money is old hat to me, unexciting although essential, neither of which it seemed in the past. I used to despise money, which could have made my old age frightening, except that writers do not retire and my earning power has increased. Sex has become like driving a car with ninety-five thousand miles on it. You don't go fast or dwell on the details but you do get there.

I know more about children, food, answering mail, theories of health, conversational tact, variants and staples of religious thought, highlights of art, and where I might like to be if a helicopter pilot were willing to lift me anywhere in the world. When I walk in the woods I carry a stick to part the brush and lend me footing in crossing a stream, but this only reminds me of African spearmen I have hiked with and makes me feel young. Beyond the memories I have, the balance and heft of a stick in my hand is primeval, as young as mankind can get.

It's a shorter journey back to my early teens, where I'll dawdle awhile with Nat King Cole. I've got the 1949 World Series on tape, Yankees versus Dodgers, the civilized banter of Red Barber and Mel Allen and the suspenseful feats of Tommy Henrich, Yogi Berra, Jackie Robinson, Preacher Roe. When I need to leave the room, I re-experience that moment of panic that I'll miss Joe DiMaggio's next at bat— and can remember the silent tears filling my eyes when the Yankees would lose a game. I had a friend who grew equally teary on behalf of the Red Sox, so I suggested we call a truce and quit teasing each other about our grief, which just made it worse. But he said no, that wouldn't be *baseball*.

I'm still loath to believe he was right, yet the evidence sits right here on the table. Besides the violin partitas and "Goldberg Variations" that occupy some of the best of my days, I've acquired a radio scanner that plugs me into the muffled shouts of out-of-breath firemen, ambulance attendants, sheriff's deputies chasing a thief, state police zeroing in on a bank robber's flight. Presumably these emergencies would hold no interest for me if gloating over another person's disappointment when his team loses were not also part of the appeal of sports.

There's malice in us till we die. I've never met an elderly person fit in his faculties who was completely benign. But the obverse of that is the incongruous picture we keep of ourselves as remaining forever around the age of eighteen. I'm startled whenever I look at my body, yet when I first strip to swim in a pond near my home, I'm nonchalant in the fashion of a quite comely youth. (So what if someone shows up? They may find me worth a glance.) In our minds lives the remnant mischief of a kid, and not only the cruel, envious, jittery goblin who will inhabit us until we drop, but a kind spirit who feels sorry for lobsters after decades of eating them, who winces at hollering voices if one is an adult's and the other a child's, and who wants to write big checks for famine relief.

Though closer to death, I am more reconciled, having seen my father, mother, ex-wife, and five or six intimate friends die rather slowly—events that were sadly cryptic but because of painkillers were no longer a terrifying mystery, scalding like hellfire, as they would have been hundreds of years ago, when hellfire was a buzzword. I don't expect to rejoin or "miss" these people in the hereafter, yet, having spent a great deal of my personal and professional life riding a surf of wind-song, wolf howls, elephants snuffling, trees soughing, grasshoppers buzzing, frogs croaking, I do think I'll mix in somehow with all of the above, the wine of human nature blending with the milk of outdoor nature in a mulligatawny soup of soil, rainwater, and pondy chemicals, with infinite possibilities once again.

Reincarnation or a heavenly life is the ultimate comfort offered by every religion I am familiar with, and I don't want to be *me* for more than another twenty years anyway. Neither eternal oblivion nor me, but something else. Maybe moss. One could do worse. Moss, if left alone, seems to live about as long as people do; then it goes back to mulligatawny soup again. Having witnessed the Sudanese famine in 1993, I expect to see other scarifying tragedies that will ease me into a grateful grave. But during my sixty-first year I also saw India on a first visit, and Antarctica—tigers and ice.

As Renaissance men of a new kind, we should feast our eyes. Instead, we fret about civilization. Civilization is with us to stay. I worry more about the toads' and the tree frogs' songs. I want that stew to be yeasty with tadpole, muskrat and other bones, loons' bills, lady slippers, skunk cabbage, jack-in-the-pulpits, and moose and bear pies, not just an ossuary of human relics. Otherwise my moss is not going to thrive.

HEAVEN
AND NATURE

A friend of mine, a peaceable soul who has been riding
the New York subways for thirty years, finds himself
stepping back from the tracks once in a while and closing
his eyes as the train rolls in. This, he says, is not only to sup-
press an urge to throw himself in front of it but because
every couple of weeks an impulse rises in him to push a
stranger onto the tracks, any stranger, thus ending his own
life too. He blames this partly on apartment living, "pigeon-
holes without being able to fly."

It is profoundly startling not to trust oneself after
decades of doing so. I don't dare keep ammunition in my
country house for a small rifle I bought secondhand two
decades ago. The gun had sat in a cupboard in the back
room with the original box of .22 bullets under the muzzle
all that time, seldom fired except at a few apples hanging in
a tree every fall to remind me of my army training near the
era of the Korean War, when I'd been considered quite a
marksman. When I bought the gun I didn't trust either my
professional competence as a writer or my competence as a
father as much as I came to, but certainly believed I could

keep myself alive. I bought it for protection, and the idea that someday I might be afraid of shooting myself with the gun would have seemed inconceivable—laughable.

One's fifties can be giddy years, as anybody fifty knows. Chest pains, back pains, cancer scares, menopausal or prostate complications are not the least of it, and the fidelities of a lifetime, both personal and professional, may be called into question. Was it a mistake to have stuck so long with one's marriage, and to have stayed with a lackluster, well-paying job? (Or *not* to have stayed and stuck?) People cannot only lose faith in their talents and dreams or values; some simply tire of them. Grow tired, too, of the smell of fried-chicken grease, once such a delight, and the cold glutinosity of ice cream, the boredom of beer, the stop-go of travel, the hiccups of laughter, and of two rush hours a day, then the languor of weekends, of athletes as well as accountants, and even the frantic birdsong of spring: red-eyed vireos that have been clocked singing twenty-two thousand times in a day. Life is a matter of cultivating the six senses, and an equilibrium with nature and what I think of as its subdivision, human nature—trusting no one completely but almost everyone at least a little. But this is easier said than done.

More than thirty thousand Americans took their own lives last year, men mostly, with the highest rate among those older than sixty-five. When I asked a friend why three times as many men kill themselves as members of her own sex, she replied with sudden anger, "I'm not going to go into the self-indulgence of men."

They won't bend to failure, she said, and want to make themselves memorable. Suicide is an exasperating act as often as it is pitiable. "Committing" suicide is in bad odor in our culture even among those who don't believe that to cash

in your chips ahead of time and hand back to God his gifts
to you is a blasphemous sin. We the living, in any case, are
likely to feel accused by this person who "voted with his
feet." It appears to cast a subversive judgment upon the
social polity as a whole that what was supposed to work in
life—religion, family, friendship, commerce, and industry—
did not, and furthermore it frightens the horses in the street,
as Shaw's friend Mrs. Patrick Campbell once defined wrong-
ful behavior.

Many suicides inflict outrageous trauma, burning permanent injuries on the minds of their children, though they
may have joked beforehand only of "taking a dive." And
sometimes the gesture has a peevish or cowardly aspect, or
seems to have been senselessly shortsighted as far as an
outside observer can tell. There are desperate suicides and
crafty suicides, people who do it to cause others trouble
and people who do it to save others trouble, deranged exhi-
bitionists who yell from a building ledge, and closemouthed,
secretive souls who swim out into the ocean's anonymity.
Suicide may in fact be an attempt to escape death, shortcut
the dreadful deteriorating processes, abort one's natural tra-
jectory, elude "the ruffian on the stairs," in A. E. Housman's
phrase for a cruelly painful, anarchic death—make it neat and
not messy. The deed can be grandiose or self-abnegating,
vindictive or drably mousy, rationally plotted or plainly
insane. People sidle toward death, intent upon outwitting
their own bodies' defenses, or they may dramatize the
chance to make one last, unambiguous, irrevocable decision, like a captain scuttling his ship—death before dis-
honor—leaping toward oblivion through a curtain of pain,
like a frog going down the throat of a snake. One man I
knew hosted a quietly affectionate evening with several

unknowing friends on the night before he swallowed too many pills. Another waved an apologetic good-bye to a bystander on a bridge. Seldom shy ordinarily, and rarely considerate, he turned shy and apologetic in the last moment of life. Never physically inclined, he made a great vault toward the ice on the Mississippi.

In the army, we wore dog tags with a notch at one end by which these numbered pieces of metal could be jammed between our teeth, if we lay dead and nameless on a battlefield, for later sorting. As "servicemen" our job would be to kill people who were pointed out to us as enemies, or make "the supreme sacrifice" for a higher good than enjoying the rest of our lives. Life was very much a possession, in other words—not only God's, but the soldier's own to dispose of. Working in an army hospital, I frequently did handle dead bodies, but this never made me feel I would refuse to kill another man whose uniform was pointed out to me as being inimical, or value my life more tremulously and vigilantly. The notion of dying for my country never appealed to me as much as dying freelance for my ideas (in the unlikely event that I *could* do that), but I was ready. People were taught during the 1940s and 1950s that one should be ready to die for one's beliefs. Heroes were revered because they had deliberately chosen to give up their lives. Life would not be worth living under the tyranny of an invader, and Nathan Hale apparently hadn't paused to wonder whether God might not have other uses for him besides being hung. Nor did the pilot Colin Kelly hesitate before plunging his plane into a Japanese battleship, becoming America's first well-publicized hero in World War II.

I've sometimes wondered why people who know that they are terminally ill, or who are headed for suicide, so very seldom have paused to take a bad guy along with them. It's lawless to consider an act of assassination, yet hardly more so, really, than suicide is regarded in some quarters (or death itself, in others). Government bureaucracies, including our own, in their majesty and as the executors of laws, regularly weigh whether or not to murder a foreign antagonist. Of course the answer is that most individuals are fortunately more timid as well as humbler in their judgment than government officialdom. But, beyond that, when dying or suicidal, they no longer care enough to devote their final energies to doing good works of any kind—Hitler himself in their gun sights they would have passed up. Some suicides become so crushed and despairing that they can't recognize the consequences of anything they do, and it's not primarily vindictiveness that wreaks such havoc upon their survivors but their derangement from ordinary life.

Courting the idea is different from the real impulse. "When he begged for help, we took him and locked him up," another friend of mine says, speaking of her husband. "Not till then. Wishing to be out of the situation you are in—feeling helpless and unable to cope—is not the same as wishing to be dead. If I actually wished to be dead, even my children's welfare would have no meaning."

You might think the ready option of divorce available lately would have cut suicide rates, offering an escape to battered wives, lovelorn husbands, and other people in despair. But it doesn't work that way. When the number of choices people have increases, an entire range of possibilities opens up. Suicide among teenagers has almost quadrupled since

1950, although the standard of comfort that their families enjoy is up. Black Americans, less affluent than white Americans, have had less of a rise in suicides, and the rate among them remains about half of that for whites.

Still, if a fiftyish fellow with fine teeth and a foolproof pension plan, a cottage at the beach, and the Fourth of July weekend coming up kills himself, it seems truculent. We would look at him in bafflement if he told us he no longer likes the Sturm und Drang of banging fireworks.

Then stay at your hideaway! we'd argue with him.

"Big mouths eat little mouths. Nature isn't 'timeless.' Whole lives are squeezed into three months or three days."

What about your marriage?

"She's become more mannish than me. I loved women. I don't believe in marriage between men."

Remarry, then!

"I've gone impotent, and besides, when I see somebody young and pretty I guess I feel like dandling her on my knee."

Marriage is friendship. You can find someone your own age.

"I'm tired of it."

But how about your company? A widows-and-orphans stock that's on the cutting edge of the silicon frontier? That's interesting.

"I know what wins. It's less and less appetizing."

You're not scared of death anymore?

"It interests me less than it did."

What are you so sick of? The rest of us keep going.

"I'm tired of weathermen and sportscasters on the screen. Of being patient and also of impatience. I'm tired of the president, whoever the president happens to be, and sleeping badly, with forty-eight half-hours in the day—of breaking two eggs every morning and putting sugar on something. I'm tired of the drone of my own voice, but also of us jabbering like parrots at each other—of all our stumpy ways of doing everything."

You're bored with yourself?

"That's an understatement. I'm maybe the least interesting person I know."

But to kill yourself?

"You know, it's a tradition, too," he remarks quietly, not making so bold as to suggest that the tradition is an honorable one, though his tone of voice might be imagined to imply this. "I guess I've always been a latent maverick."

Except in circumstances which are themselves a matter of life and death, I'm reluctant to agree with the idea that suicide is not the result of mental illness. No matter how reasonably the person appears to have examined his options, it goes against the grain of nature for him to destroy himself. But any illness that threatens his life then changes a person. Suicidal thinking, if serious, can be a kind of death scare, comparable to suffering a heart attack or undergoing a cancer operation. One survives such a phase both warier and chastened. When—ten years ago—I emerged from a bad dip into suicidal speculation, I felt utterly exhausted and yet quite fearless of ordinary dangers, vastly afraid of myself but much less scared of extraneous eventualities. The fact of death may not be tragic; many people die with a bit of a smile that captures their mouths at the last instant, and most people who are revived after a deadly accident are reluctant to be brought to life, resisting resuscitation, and carrying back confusing, beamish, or ecstatic memories. Yet the same impetuosity that made him throw himself out of the window might have enabled the person to love life all the more, if he'd been calibrated somewhat differently at the time of the emergency. Death's edge is so abrupt and near that many people who expect a short and momentary dive may be astounded to find that it is bottomless, and change their minds and start to scream when they are halfway down.

Although my fright at my mind's anarchy superseded my fear of death in the conventional guise of automobile or airplane crashes, heart seizures, and so on, nightmares are more primitive and in my dreams I continued to be scared of a death not sought after—dying from driving too fast and losing control of the car, breaking through thin ice while skating and drowning in the cold, or falling off a cliff. When I am tense and sleeping raggedly, my worst nightmare isn't drawn from anxious prep-school memories or my stint in the army or the bad spells of my marriages or any other of adulthood's vicissitudes. Nothing else from the past half century has the staying power in my mind of the elevated-train rides that my father and I used to take down Third Avenue to the Battery in New York City on Sunday afternoons when I was three or four or five, so I could see the fish at the aquarium. We were probably pretty good companions in those years, but the wooden platforms forty feet up shook terribly as trains from both directions pulled in and out. To me they seemed worse than rickety—ready to topple. And the roar was fearful, and the railings left large gaps for a child to fall through, after the steep climb up the slat-sided, windy, shaking stairway from street level. It's a rare dream, but several times a year I still find myself on such a perch, without his company or anybody else's, on a boyish mission, when the elevated platform begins to rattle desperately, seesaw, heel over, and finally come apart, disintegrate, while I cling to struts and trusses.

My father, as he lay dying at home of bowel cancer, used to enjoy watching Tarzan reruns on the children's hour of television. Like a strong green vine, they swung him far away from his deathbed to a world of skinny-dipping and friendly animals and scenic beauty linked to the lost realities of his adolescence in Kansas City. Earlier, when he had still been able to walk without much pain, he'd paced the house for several hours at night, contemplating suicide, I expect, along with other anguishing thoughts, regrets, remembrances, and yearnings, while the rest of us slept. But he decided to lie down and die the slower way. I don't know how much of that decision was because he didn't want to be a "quitter," as he sometimes put it, and how much was due to his believing that life belongs to God (which I'm not even sure he did). He was not a churchgoer after his thirties. He had belonged to J. P. Morgan's church, Saint George's, on Stuyvesant Square in Manhattan—Morgan was a hero of his. But when things went a little wrong for him at the Wall Street law firm he worked for, and he changed jobs and moved out to the suburbs, he became a skeptic on religious matters, and gradually, in the absence of faith of that previous kind, adhered to a determined allegiance to the social order. Wendell Willkie or Dwight D. Eisenhower, instead of J. P. Morgan, became the sort of hero he admired, and suicide would have seemed an act of insurrection against the laws and conventions of the internationalist-Republican society that he believed in.

I was never particularly afraid that I might plan a suicide, swallowing a bunch of pills and keeping them down— only of what I think of as Anna Karenina's kind of death.

This most plausible self-killing in all literature is frightening because it was unwilled, regretted at midpoint, and came as a complete surprise to Anna herself. After rushing impulsively, in great misery, to the railway station to catch a train, she ended up underneath another one, dismayed, astonished, and trying to climb out from under the wheels, even as they crushed her. Many people who briefly verge on suicide undergo a mental somersault for a terrifying interval during which they're upside down, their perspective topsyturvy, skidding, churning; and this is why I got rid of the bullets for my .22.

Nobody expects to trust his body overmuch after the age of fifty. Incipient cataracts or arthritis, outlandish snores, tooth grinding, ankles that threaten to turn are part of the game. But not to trust one's *mind?* That's a surprise. The single attribute that older people were sure to have (we thought as boys) was a stodgy dependability, a steady temperance or caution. Adults might be vain, unimaginative, pompous, and callous, but they did have their affairs tightly in hand. It was not till my thirties that I began to know friends who were in their fifties on equal terms, and I remember being amused, piqued, irritated, and slightly bewildered to learn that some of them still felt as marginal or rebellious or in a quandary about what to do with themselves for the next dozen years as my contemporaries were likely to. That close to retirement, some of them harbored a deep-seated contempt for the organizations they had been working for, being ready to walk away from almost everybody they had known, and the efforts and expertise of whole decades, with very little sentiment. Nor did twenty years of marriage necessarily mean more than two or three—they might be just as ready to walk away from that also, and didn't really register it as twenty or thirty years at all. Rather, life could be about to begin all over again. "Bummish" was how one man described himself, with a raffish smile—"Lucky to have a roof over my head"—though he'd just put a child through Yale. He was quitting his job and claimed with exasperation that his wife still cried for her mother in her sleep, as if they'd never been married.

The great English traveler Richard Burton quoted an Arab proverb that speaks for many middle-aged men of the old-fashioned variety: "Conceal thy Tenets, thy Treasure, and thy Traveling." These are serious matters, in other words. People didn't conceal their tenets in order to betray them, but to fight for them more opportunely. And except for kings and princelings, concealing whatever treasure one had went almost without saying. As for travel, a man's travels were also a matter of gravity. Travel was knowledge, ambiguity, dalliances or misalliances, divided loyalty, forbidden thinking; and besides, someday he might need to make a run for it and go to ground someplace where he had made some secret friends. Friends of mine whose husbands or wives have died have been quite startled afterward to discover caches of money or traveler's checks concealed around the house, or a bundle of cash in a safe-deposit box.

Burton, like any other desert adage-spinner and most individuals over fifty, would have agreed to an addition so obvious that it wasn't included to begin with: "Conceal thy Illnesses." I can remember how urgently my father worried that word would get out, after a preliminary operation for his cancer. He didn't want to be written off, counted out of the running at the corporation he worked for and in other enclaves of competition. Men often compete with one another until the day they die; comradeship consists of rub-

bing shoulders jocularly with a competitor. As breadwinners, they must be considered fit and sound by friend as
well as foe, and so there's lots of truth to the most common
answer I heard when asking why three times as many men
as women kill themselves: "They don't know how to ask for
help." Men greet each other with a sock on the arm, women
with a hug, and the hug wears better in the long run.

I'm not entirely like that; and I discovered when I con-
fided something of my perturbation to a woman friend she
was likely to keep telephoning me or mailing cheery post-
cards, whereas a man would usually listen with concern,
communicate his sympathy, and maybe intimate that he had
pondered the same drastic course of action himself a few
years back and would end up respecting my decision either
way. Open-mindedness seems an important attribute to a
good many men, who pride themselves on being objective,
hearing all sides of an issue, on knowing that truth and honesty do not always coincide with social dicta, and who may
even cherish a subterranean outlaw streak that, like being
ready to violently defend one's family, reputation, and country, is by tradition male.

Men, being so much freer than women in society, used
to feel they had less of a stake in the maintenance of certain
churchly conventions and enjoyed speaking irreverently
about various social truisms, including the principle that
people ought to die on schedule, not cutting in ahead of
their assigned place in line. But contemporary women, after
their triumphant irreverence during the 1960s and 1970s,
cannot be generalized about so easily. They turn as skeptical
and saturnine as any man. In fact, women attempt suicide
more frequently, but favor pills or other passive methods,
whereas two-thirds of the men who kill themselves have

used a gun. In 1996, 87 percent of suicides by means of firearms were done by men. An overdose of medication hasn't the same finality. It may be reversible, if the person is discovered quickly, or be subject to benign miscalculation to start with. Even if it works, it can be fudged by a kindly doctor in the record keeping. Like an enigmatic drowning or a single-car accident that baffles the suspicions of the insurance company, a suicide by drugs can be a way to avoid making a loud statement, and merely illustrate the final modesty of a person who didn't wish to ask for too much of the world's attention.

Unconsummated attempts at suicide can strike the rest of us as self-pitying and self-aggrandizing, however, or like plaintive plea bargaining. "Childish," we say, though actually the suicide of children is ghastly beyond any stunt of self-mutilation an adult may indulge in because of the helplessness that echoes through the act. It would be hard to define chaos better than as a world where children decide that they don't want to live.

Love is the solution to all dilemmas, we sometimes hear. And in those moments when the spirit bathes itself in beneficence and manages to transcend the static of personalities rubbing fur off each other, indeed it is. Without love nothing matters, Paul told the Corinthians, a mystery which, if true, has no ready Darwinian explanation. Love without a significant sexual component and for people who are unrelated to us serves little practical purpose. It doesn't help us feed our families, win struggles, thrive and prosper. It distracts us from the ordinary business of sizing people up and making a living, and is not even conducive to intellectual observation, because instead of seeing them, we see right through them to the bewildered child and dreaming adolescent who

35

inhabited their bodies earlier, the now-tired idealist who fell in and out of love, got hired and quit, hired and fired, bought cars and wore them out, liked black-eyed Susans, blueberry muffins, and roosters crowing—liked roosters crowing better than skyscrapers but now likes skyscrapers better than roosters crowing. As swift as thought, we select the details that we need to see in order to be able to love them.

Yet at other times we'll dispense with these same poignancies and choose only their grunginess to look at, their pinched mouths and shifty eyes, their thirst for gin at noon and indifference to their kids, their greed for the best tidbit on the buffet table and penchant for poking their penises up the excretory end of other human beings. I tend to gaze quite closely at the faces of priests I meet on the street to see if a lifetime of love has marked them noticeably. Real serenity or asceticism I no longer expect, and I take for granted the beefy calm that frequently goes with Catholic celibacy, but I am watching for the marks of love and often see mere resignation or tenacity.

Many men are romantics—likely to plunge, go for broke, take action in a spirit of exigency rather than waiting for the problem to resolve itself. Then, on the contrary, still as romantics, they may drift into a despairing passivity, stare at the TV all day long, and binge with a bottle. Women too may turn frenetic for a while and then throw up their hands. But though they may not seem as grandiosely fanciful and romantic at the outset, they are more often believers—at least I think they tend to believe in God or in humanity, the future, and so on. We have above us the inviting eternity of "the heavens," if we choose to look at it, lying on our backs in the summer grass under starlight, some of which had left its source before mankind became man. But because we live in our heads more than in nature nowadays, even the summer sky is a minefield for people whose memories are mined. With the sky no longer humbling, the sunshine only a sort of convenience, and no godhead located anywhere outside our own heads, every problem may seem insolubly interlocked. When the telephone has become impossible to answer at home, sometimes it finally becomes impossible to stride down the gangplank of a cruise ship in Mombasa too, although no telephones will ring for you there.

But if escapist travel is ruled out in certain emergencies, surely you can *pray?* Pray, yes; but to whom? That requires a bit of preparation. Rarely do people obtain much relief from praying if they haven't stood in line awhile to get a visa. It's an appealing idea that you can just *go*, and in a previous era perhaps you could have, like on an old-fashioned shooting safari. But it's not so simple now. What do you believe in? Whom are you praying to? What are you praying for? There's no crèche on the courthouse lawn; you're not supposed to adhere exactly even to what your parents had believed. Like psychotherapy, praying takes time, even if you know which direction to face when you kneel.

Love is powerfully helpful when the roof falls in—loving other people with a high and hopeful heart and as a kind of prayer. Yet that feat too requires new and sudden insights or long practice. The beatitude of loving strangers as well as friends—loving them on sight with a leap of empathy and intuition—is a form of inspiration, edging, of course, in some cases toward madness, as other states of beatitude can do. But there's no question that a genuine love for the living will stymie suicidal depressions which are not chemical in origin. Love is an elixir, changing the life of the lover like no other. And many of us have experienced this—a temporary lightening of our leery, prickly disapproval of much of the rest of the world when at a wedding or a funeral of shared emotion, or when we have fallen in love.

Yet the zest for life of those unusual men and women who make a great zealous success of living is due more often in good part to the craftiness and pertinacity with which they manage to overlook the misery of others. You can watch them watch life beat the stuffing out of the faces of their friends and acquaintances, although they themselves seem to outwit the dense delays of social custom, the tedious tick-tock of bureaucratic obfuscation, accepting loss and age and change and disappointment without suffering punctures in their stomach lining. Breathlessness or strange dull pains from their nether organs don't nonplus them. They fret and doubt in moderation, and love a lobster roast, squeeze lemon juice on living clams on the half shell to prove that the clams are alive, laugh as robins tussle a worm out of the ground or a kitten flees a dog. Like the problem drinkers, pork eaters, and chain-smokers who nevertheless finish out their allotted years, succumbing to a stroke at a nice round biblical age while the best vitamin-eating vegetarian has long since died, their faces become veritable walnuts of fine character, with the same smile lines as the rarer individual whose grin has been affectionate all of his life.

We spend our lives getting to know ourselves, yet wonders never cease. During my adolescent years my states of mind, though undulant, seemed seamless; even when I was unhappy no cracks or fissures made me wonder if I was a danger to myself. My confidence was such that I treaded the slippery lips of waterfalls, fought forest fires, drove ancient cars cross-country night and day, and scratched the necks of menagerie leopards in the course of various adventures which enhanced the joy of being alive. The chemistry of the mind, because unfathomable, is more frightening than mere chanciness. In the city, I live on the waterfront and occasionally will notice an agitated-looking figure picking his way along the pilings and stringpieces of the timbered piers nearby, staring at the sliding whorls on the surface of the Hudson, as if teetering over an abyss. Our building, standing across the street, seems imposing from the water and over the years has acted as a magnet for a number of suicides—people who have dreaded the clammy chill, the onerous smothering essential to their first plan. One woman climbed out, after jumping in, and took the elevator to the roof (my neighbors remember how wringing wet she was) and leapt off, banging window ledges on the way down, and hit with the whap of a sack of potatoes, as others have.

Yet what is more remarkable than that a tiny minority of souls reach a point where they entrust their bodies to the force of gravity is that so few of the rest of us will splurge an hour of a summer day gazing at the trees and sky. How many summers do we *have?* One sees prosperous families in the city who keep plants in their apartment windows that have grown so high they block the sunlight and appear to be doing the living for the tenants who are bolted inside. But beauty is nobody's sure salvation: not the beauty of a swimming hole if you get a cramp, and not the beauty of a woman if she doesn't care for you. The swimming hole looks inviting under the blue sky, with its amber bottom, green sedges sticking up in the shallows, and curls of gentle current over a waterlogged birch tree two feet beneath the surface, near the brook that feeds it. Come back at dusk, however, and the pond turns black—as dark as death—or on the contrary, a restful dark, a dark to savor. Take it as you will.

People with sunny natures do seem to live longer than people who are nervous wrecks; yet mankind didn't evolve out of the animal kingdom by being unduly sunny-minded. Life was fearful and phantasmagoric, supernatural and preternatural, as well as encompassing the kind of clockwork regularity of our well-governed day. It had numerous superstitious (from the Latin, "standing over") elements, such as we are likely to catch a whiff of only when we're peering at a dead body. And it was not just our optimism but our pessimistic premonitions, our dark moments as a species, our irrational, frightful speculations, our strange mutations upon the simple theme of love, and our sleepless, obsessive inventiveness—our dread as well as our faith—that made us human beings. Staking one's life on the more general good came to include risking suicide also. Brilliant, fecund people sometimes kill themselves.

Joy to the world. . . . Let heaven and nature sing. . . . Repeat the sounding joy . . . The famous Christmas carol invokes not only glee but unity: heaven with nature, not always a Christian combination. It's a rapturous hymn, and no one should refuse to surrender to such a pitch of revelation when it comes. But the flip side of rapture can be a riptide of panic, of hysterical gloom. Our faces are not molded as if joy were a preponderant experience. (Nor is a caribou's or a thrush's.) Our faces in repose look stoic or battered, and people of the sunniest temperament sometimes die utterly unstrung, doubting everything they have ever believed in or have done.

Let heaven and nature sing! the hymn proclaims. But *is* there such harmony? Are God and Mother Nature really the same? Are they even compatible? And will we risk burning our wings if we mount high enough to try to see? I've noticed that woods soil in Italy smells the same as woods soil in New England, when you pick up a handful of it and enjoy its aroma. But is God there the same? It can be precarious to wonder.

I don't rule out suicide as being unthinkable for people who have tried to live full lives; and don't regard it as negating the work and faith and satisfaction and fun and even ecstasy they may have known before. In killing himself a person acknowledges his failures during a time span when perhaps heaven and earth had caught him like a pair of scissors—but doesn't repudiate his life span. Man is different from animals in that he speculates, a high-risk activity.

RUNNING MATES

Many people will kiss an animal—their dog or cat—
more often during the course of a day than they'll
kiss a human being. Morning, noon, or night, they'll bestow
the most demonstrative affection on some furry surrogate (I
do it, too), more than the animal really appears to want. Its
acquiescence in these hugs and kisses is part of how it pays
its way. And this state of affairs, I suspect, is only becoming
more pervasive, as E-mail and telephone friendships replace
face-to-face contact and as we also lose our links to outdoor
nature, making domestic pets serve emotional uses they seldom would have had on a working farm. Tender One; the
Child That Never Was; or ersatz hunting partner, as we walk
along the street. We may fight with a spouse and stroke the
dog at the same time. See, *he* loves me! As life gets ever more
wired, we're comforted that a dependent animal is always
home, always hands-on, not just another voice-mail friend.

Friends are not much less essential than food. In adolescence one had "best" friends: such constant confiding was
necessary about our secrets and sorrows, panic attacks, and
peaks of satisfaction. And in the exigencies of divorce, for

example, friends sometimes again become not just a loose web of alliances at work or chums for the weekend, but urgent midnight confidants. As in adolescence, you count on certain people or else get mad at them because they "failed" you. We have old friends, work friends, school-board friends, lovers who may have stayed friends, friends of friends that we stay with in San Diego, TV personalities we probably spend more time with than most of the above, and sudden, fleeting seatmate intimacies that luck or circumstance toss to us. Some friendships are the meat-and-potatoes type, others tart or sweet: hash and eggs, poached salmon, or blueberry pancakes. Or you'll meet a hearty business trade-off guy for lunch who suggests if you do this or that for him, he might do the same for you.

Familiar stuff; and so much so that a shorthand will often suffice. One eases one's heart with friends, but gradually one ceases to expect miracles—the amazing romance, the professional boost, the revelation in a coffeehouse. We know our discontents are not to be as simply solved. Our talents will remain puddled about our feet, just as they were before, and our regrets half-unearthed and therefore unassuaged. We know the cards each person has dealt himself (I tend to believe in free will), and so we catch up by asking him about his kids, health, job, or matters that come under the heading of petty politics. A new friend, like a spare suit, won't make a new man of you.

Yet various deaths start chiming in—good friends—as you grow older. A thinning crew, the quick and the dead, inhabits your head. It's dissonant and alarming. As if instinctively, I seem to make a point of finding a prospective new friend after every death, but when you're past sixty, your intensity of involvement with any acquaintance is not likely to be a match for the affection that has been lost. Most of us do get more tolerant as we leave behind the hectic fracases of breadwinning in middle age, however; we can afford to. And we're likely to be more accurate in sizing up a stranger. Somewhere along the line, we've seen his twin. But we are also less interested and more dismissive. Our juices do not percolate in company with the same hope or zest. We know the patterns people fall into and don't expect to be surprised. Though we accept these individuals as valid variants on the human model without quibbling too much that they differ from us, we've seen so many our curiosity is limited. Not villains or traitors or scam-men populate the world: just ordinary, evasive, self-absorbed persons hamstrung by modest miscues committed years ago, like us.

I've lost no friends to war or accidents, only to disease. One strangled slowly in the same way Lou Gehrig did. Another died of prostate cancer that might have been arrested sooner if he had gone to see a doctor. He was a newspaperman, proud to have sprung from a Brooklyn longshore family that always went to chiropractors for their aches and pains. But this time spinal manipulation didn't help. Another succumbed to bowel cancer, another to cancer of the throat, both early deaths genetically programmed from family history. The latter was a Classics teacher and right up to the end kept enlightening his nurse with quips regarding mythic characters or language etymology, whatever popped into his mind. Several others drank and smoked too soon, too long, too much, having fallen for the romantic notions of the postwar era drawn from Kafka, existentialism, Beckett, or the Beats, which dictated that life was supposed to be insupportable. Even if it wasn't, you drank, smoked, and did drugs a lot in order to pretend that it was, or burned the candle at both ends to be like folk of a different stripe, a Dostoyevsky or a Scott Fitzgerald. Of course some people were genuinely impaled upon conundrums not of their choosing—a simmering anguish that, when you went to write a memorial tribute to them and called up mutual friends, everybody agreed that, "Yes, *something* happened to him when he was little, but I don't know what it was."

Two killed themselves. John Berryman jumped onto the ice of the Mississippi at fifty-seven, out of mental illness; and my high-school writing teacher, Richard Hatch, jumped into the Atlantic when he was in his eighties and going deaf and blind. My own closest brush with suicide was during the three years I spent legally blind. Though surgery eventually corrected the problem, it felt a bit like being terminally ill, and the friendships I emerged from that experience with are the connections I value most now. A pizzeria owner here in my town in Vermont, who from the goodness of his heart drove me around when I had to get places but couldn't see, is still the man I chat with most frequently. I trust him and we came to understand one another. On my side, I helped him sort through a charnel house of combat memories from Korea and, before that, a childhood where his father threw his mother down the cellar stairs and punished him by nailing him under the slatted back-porch stoop.

The idea of a previous life one leaves behind has become commonplace, with divorce, psychotherapy, cross-country career changes, housing shifts, and other forms of flux. Jack be nimble, Jill be quick are the watchwords now for people who aim to move up, rather than the reputation for honesty and consistency that mattered in my parents' generation. Only classmates at a college reunion may recognize what-

ever constancy underlies their costume colorations. People
jump about so much emotionally and geographically that a
new sort of currency attaches to friendship. Not just the old
notion of having useful cronies to make advantageous intro-
ductions, but more provisionally: *while* I'm here. The temporary hometown; this year's roost.

My father, a conventional sort of man rooted in the
pieties of his time, left token bequests to his church and
country club because they'd been lifetime resorts, like two
legs of a tripod. Nevertheless, I remember his alarm when
he was first diagnosed with cancer that the news would get
out to his colleagues and put a sudden kibosh on the third
leg, which was his legal career. A sick friend is a different
kind of colleague, and he was afraid his professional pals
would be solicitous but immediately begin writing him off,
that they would stop regarding him as a player and a heavy
lifter before he was actually gone. And when my turn came
and I went blind and couldn't write effectively or review
books, jury literary contests, function in the bookish marketplace, or recommend other writers for fellowships and
teaching jobs, I remembered how apprehensive he had
been. After thirty or forty years in the running, I seemed
out. I was no longer to be reckoned with, and a number
of friends and acquaintances dropped me very promptly,
though they picked me up again after my surgeon had
brought me back from oblivion.

It can make you a cynic, but, on the other hand, pets do
not suffice for company; nor religion. My own deity is imma-
nent, not manlike, not a guy you can pray to. Yet even Jeho-
vah will come up short if you lack people to rub shoulders
and press the flesh with, say what the weather's like and
how-are-you. Friends are leverage; we need some traction,

some footing. "Bless you!" they say if we sneeze. When we are young we are inventing the wheel and need a best friend to pour our hearts out to, so very much requires expression. Later we shed this phase, as different friends turn out to be more suited for sharing different experiences and less urgency rides on each conversation.

We're looking for running mates—people to raise kids and joke about going gray with. I have five or six close friends located in separate places whom I could tell practically anything to, but rarely do. One learns there's nothing earthshaking to tell. For instance, when somebody complains once too often about the weather, I tell them that every day is a good day, the fundamental lesson I learned when I was blind. But this is nothing they haven't heard a hundred times before from a representative of one of the world's organized religions. And though I tend to prefer the companionship of women to men, the five or six close friends I am referring to are men, because the deeper, riskier intimacy of living with a woman sometimes precludes the promiscuity of total, casual confidences. Too much is at stake if you are sharing your whole life with somebody and might miscalculate their reaction.

My mother used to say she didn't believe disinterested friendship was possible between men and women: that is, where no sexual attraction existed. And I suppose (excepting kind hearts) some glimmer of lubricity does need to be factored in with friends of different genders, an illicit whisper of hang-fire romance—the seashell of an ear, the twitch of a neck, as if the lady's hair still hung in a ponytail, and her wry disciplinary air if you stare too long at her, as though she's still ready to seize a wandering hand. It's a double-decker friendship, echoic and androgynous, with landscaped walls and ha-has, speed bumps and baffles, that homosexual men and women enjoy as well because they complicate and thus enhance unserious flirtation, whereas a true former lover who is allowed to continue to frequent the house may appear bound and gagged. Same-sex friendships can of course also have a sexual component, but are not almost certain to.

Friendship can be exploitive and predatory, a strange symbiosis of quiet underwater carnage, though I've seldom seen one stay that way. Yet friends *are* partly for quarreling with. Most of us need to squabble occasionally in order to tap off our toxins, and friends permit us to without inflammatory consequences. We can be a trifle mean, or stumble into a brief tailspin, and be forgiven. Knowing our knotty nuttiness, our self-destructive lonely spells, they let us phone a bit too much and don't require us to specify just how tricky we feel. Friends are for jitters as well as barbecues.

But I know a woman who keeps track of fifty friends by E-mail every morning when she logs onto her computer. This seems extreme to me. I wouldn't mind knowing fifty people I could call friends—but not their daily whereabouts and preoccupations. I'm content with weekly or even bimonthly updates because often the sweetest aspect of old friendships is how incredibly little people seem to change. Same funky smarts and savvy sympathy, same pessimistic grin and hunchy scuttle. These don't fully show on the computer, and in the meantime I don't have to know whenever their kids play soccer or they swallow a couple of aspirin and close a febrile deal.

Maybe I'm a Luddite on this matter. Cyberspace may be precisely how people will remain able to function (that and an explosion of pets) in a leapfrog world where nobody sees much of anybody in the flesh, except for a serial spouse. My century was the twentieth; it was my job to learn to swim in the currents of that, and my present usefulness does not relate to whether I work by kerosene lamp, typewriter, or digitry. I have several friends who, though married to the same wife for more than a quarter of a century, have stayed sexually faithful and profoundly rooted in their communities, who serve on the planning commission or teach, take in foster children, do nursing, and see their parents and in-laws frequently. The rhythm in their houses, when you visit, is different, like a pendulum clock with Latin numerals on its face, which, wound once a month, lasts for a hundred years.

Friendship isn't a novel invention. You give me vitamins; I'll give you minerals. You give me understanding; I'll give you patience. You stand up for me and I'll argue loyally on your behalf. You remember my history, and I'll remember yours, even if you happen to die first and there's no further trade-off. People that charge two hundred dollars an hour to talk with clients will chat for free with their friends. Simply to survive we need each other; it's a barter arrangement. Not money but memories are what we die with, and memories are composed of images of other people. My mother's, as she lay slowly dying of a series of strokes, were drawn from her halcyon years when she was in her teens and again in her forties, she told me. Friends you choose, and they aren't like love affairs, where timing, as the old saw goes, is everything. When friends marry, you can keep on seeing them. If your breasts and belly sag, you don't lose a friend. Nor do you rush to change your shirt when a friend drops in.

Friends are free, like the sun. Not much rent to pay, and no real peril is involved. Friendship is fluid. A friend is not a spouse or a boss, and you can quit without losing your source of income or spending the next decade recuperating from the trauma. If we ever do put into practice the Golden Rule, it's likely to be with our friends. We're better with them than with subordinates; we can't be fired because of their miscues. And we're less unbending or hypocritical, less compulsive and irrational, than with our children or our own parents. We don't steer or punish, placate or reward our friends nearly as much. And they don't scar us for life if they betray us, as our parents can; nor we them, as we might, perhaps, our children.

We want to see our friends flower in the various ways that they think best. If they long to be rich, we want them rich. If they wish to be clever, we want them clever. If they desire integrity with obscurity, we want them unfamous and honorable. Common decency is the coin of the realm that we expect to share with them. A bad misunderstanding, like a loan that isn't paid back, we'll chalk up to experience. We don't generally fly our intimate friends like pennants on a yacht that summarize our standing—or cherish them as missives to posterity, like grandchildren. Instead, we muddle through the middle territory of life with their assistance. Heroics are for solitaries. Friends are for the rest of us.

STEPPING BACK

In the goblin world of childhood, I wished to be accepted and yet not cowardly. Handicapped by a bad stutter, I walked on coals much of the day and had enough problems without misbehaving and compounding them. My sins therefore were mostly of omission. I cried, for instance, from an access of nerves while boxing with a smaller boy at age eight before an audience of parents at a fancy imitation-British school in Manhattan, Saint Bernard's, where some of our "masters," I remember (this was 1940), threw chalk at us if we acted up in class.

That summer, again, I behaved in a way that worried me. I was walking down a path in the country with a bunch of other kids when my dog, Flash, ranging ahead, killed a farmer's chicken. Instead of manfully staying to face the music, I turned tail in utter panic and ran. Then after a minute, remembering that the dog might be caught and punished—and surprised that the other children hadn't done the same—I screwed up my nerve enough to go back, where I found them negotiating and apologizing for me, and the farmer willing to forgive my cowardice only on account of my age.

I remember crying again quite publicly at fourteen from an attack of jitters on my first day at boarding school, when I couldn't locate my assigned table in the crowded dining hall and was afraid to ask. With my stutter, I had been paired to room with a Chicago boy who suffered from asthma and needed to carry an inhaler. But what happened, toward winter, in our cruelly casuistical dorm, is that he came to be picked on and I didn't. On the face of it, he fit the mold of our particular school better than I, and his troubles stopped the next year, with different friends in a new building.

Our vulnerability in each case was of the push-button variety. That is, he would gasp or I would stutter right on cue if bullied. But mine was a constant problem, more frequent than his asthma and often with no obvious cause. Thus maybe his seemed predictable and physical, whereas mine appeared to be emotional or mental and therefore mysterious or even "catching." Or possibly my long habituation to a secret underlying conviction of helplessness had made me more elusive and manipulative. Asthma did not entail elaborate diplomacy with teachers in order not to be called upon in class; with friends, to seem companionable although forced to sit silent; with strangers, to prevent impromptu episodes of embarrassment; and with enemies, to forestall sadism. Indeed, as Billy Budd learned, a stutterer had best enkindle no enemies at all.

By whatever tactics (a good deal later, in the army, I was called the Smiler, the Whistler, Slim, or Doc), our corridor crowd accepted my condition. But every evening after study hour, several mean guys would congregate outside the room, snickering and giggling, and storm in to force a desperate wrestling match upon my roommate until he started wheezing so badly that he collapsed on the couch and had to use his inhaler. Satisfied with their power, they'd quickly leave, but this continued so invariably through the winter, the wonder is he didn't despair and quit the school.

I was agitated, horrified, fascinated, sympathetic, but I did nothing, which was the popular position as well as cowardly. Instead of making common cause with him against his tormentors, I stepped back and let him fight alone, to try to keep in the good graces of the majority. Not liking this, I gradually found friends elsewhere, as he did, and we ceased hanging out together. But the memory bothers me. Forty years afterward, I obtained his address from the alumni office and wrote to ask his forgiveness. Haven't heard a word.

By that point in adolescence I had begun to encounter the distinction between cowardice that is popular and cowardice that is not. At home in the suburbs in the late 1940s, for example, anti-Semitism was rampant and ascendant, not to mention color prejudice—tennis and golf as played at country clubs are forever linked in my memory with these. And because the empathy for underdogs that my stutter had instilled in me soon kicked in, I hated the bland, exclusive affluence of our club's flagstoned patios. But to argue social justice with my parents was only natural—an easy win for righteousness against people I was supposed to argue with. To stand up to the conventional wisdom of my privileged contemporaries took more gumption. Generally I chose the sidelong method of writing instead of saying what I thought, but I spoke enough to have been called a "Commie" on several occasions by my middle teens.

We seldom learn for sure that we're not cowards, however, because our commitments fluctuate, and in the meantime we may act with a wrongheaded foolhardiness that later turns us toward caution. I don't believe that one can live fully if one is too afraid of dying (as in, for instance, being overly fearful of lightning, hurricanes, earthquakes, or flying), and I was comfortable as a soldier in the 1950s. But I had achieved an earlier sense of equanimity during the summer when I was twenty and fought fires in the mountains of the California Coast Range for the U.S. Forest Service. I didn't have to talk fluently, just help to chop a fire line.

Fire cannot burn bare ground or whatever has already been blackened, though with the wind as its ally it can run uphill through brush much faster than a man. So you must be able to watch a fire burn without fighting it, if it is likely to entrap you—otherwise your days of being intrepid are numbered. These simple rules are paradigms I carried with me into the army, then to Africa as a roving journalist, and later to the internecine matrix of academia and literary politics. With a little flexibility, they continued to apply.

I remember a boy of about eight, with a face that reminded me of mine when I was a child, who gazed out the window of a rubbernecker's car as I stepped into the woods in the blaze of a big forest fire. His face was all alight with romance and admiration for me. But bravery may more realistically be described as knowing when to fight—and cowardice, as not.

A PEACEABLE
KINGDOM

———◆———

It's too good to be true, I've always thought, for the past thirty years, when spring rolls around once again and I drive up to my warm-weather home, now the only occupied house on a four-mile stretch of dirt road that crosses a mountain notch in northeastern Vermont. A two-story frame dwelling, painted blue-gray and nearly a hundred years old, it was built by the first family who cleared these sparse fields. They had forty acres, ten or twelve cows, and three other families for neighbors, two living in log cabins that have since fallen in—enough kids altogether for a one-room school, which later was moved next door as a shell, when *that* family's original house burned and they needed a new one.

My predecessors, too, had thrown together a log cabin at first; a barge-shaped depression in the woods still marks where it stood. Then when they decided to stay, they dug a cellar hole here with a horse-drawn scoop, split some granite boulders at the base of the cliff for blocks of stone to line it with, and set up a little sawmill to cut floorboards of spruce. Sand from the stream was used for the plastering, and they planted apple trees and a black cherry tree, and four oaks, now nice and big, in front.

The farming ceased about forty years ago. The man I bought the house from was supporting himself by brewing corn whiskey and bathtub beer and shooting deer out of season for meat. He died too soon from drinking too much, and his British war-bride wife afterward, though she was a favorite person of mine and planted many of the flower beds I continue to enjoy. The lack of electric and phone lines had made them eager to move, and indeed explains why this mountain road has never been as unpopulated as it is now, and why beyond my house it is being abandoned "to the Indians," as the town authorities say.

What I do when I arrive is air and sweep the house, load the wood stove, turn the water pipe on (it runs by gravity from a cistern uphill), browse my bookshelves for a glimpse of old friends, and check to see if the local ermine has spent the winter inside, clearing the place of the few pairs of white-footed mice that otherwise might have chewed my socks. I prefer to find her hairy little twists of dung over anybody else's. Chipmunks, when they wake from semi-hibernation, may have sought entry, too.

I open the four bird boxes that hang on trees to clear out squirrel nests (if any red squirrels have sheltered there through the snowy months), hoping that now tree swallows will come instead, and climb into the hayloft of the barn to see if a bear slept out the season in the mounds of hay, or merely some raccoons. I also look for the phoebes, early arrivals that nest under my eaves, then listen for white-throated sparrows, ovenbirds, yellowthroats, wood thrushes, robins, winter wrens, rose-breasted grosbeaks, chestnut-sided warblers, mourning warblers, and black-throated green, black-throated blue, and black-and-white warblers. Cedar waxwings, indigo buntings, flickers, and goldfinches will be arriving. A certain apple-tree limb is where the hummingbirds will nest.

If the large mother coon has survived the winter, she will probably be using the hollow maple as a den tree. By putting my ear next to it, I may hear her kits. The ermine (now an ordinary brown weasel) that protected my woolens has meanwhile moved from the house to nest among the timbers of the barn. Investigating clues perhaps left by the adolescent bear in the hayloft, I'll hear her burbling expressions of alarm. The mother woodchuck hibernates under the chicken coop and reappears as soon as the grass does; and if I'm lucky, I'll see a migrating trio of black ducks sneak in at dusk for a night's rest—out of the hurly-burly of the lakes nearby—in my high-up, hidden frog pond. They'll eat some water greens at dawn, and then be gone. Bears will have already clipped off the young spring sedges at water level. Sedges are among the first foods bears taste; or they trudge to the fir woods a few hundred yards downhill, where some deer have generally wintered, to find out if any died. I look for antlers the living bucks have dropped, but bears sniff for a carcass they can eat, though they will gobble deer droppings, too, in this hungry time, and search for last fall's sprouted beechnuts on the ground.

The lawn under my oaks, mossy and mushroomy, doesn't need much mowing. The apple trees mainly feed the wildlife, and I bush hog the fields only often enough to keep them open. The stream was dammed seventy-five years ago for homegrown experiments with water power, but flows just as it wishes now, and moose, deer, and coyotes drink from it instead of cows. I sometimes do, too, or kingfishers, ravens, or woodcock make use of it, and a great blue heron hunts mice and frogs alongside. I had the frog pond dug, hiring a bulldozer for the purpose of filling the air with song. Spring peepers and wood frogs start up in April. Then tree frogs, green frogs, pickerel frogs, and of course toads—my favorite serenaders of all—join in. As the lush orchard grass and the thick raspberry patch sloping away from the old barn have lost their soil nutrients from half a century's worth of cow manure from the animals that were stabled there, fireweed and other hardscrabble plants replaced them and what had been a teeming colony of earthworms became scarcer. This was tough on the colony of garter snakes living underneath my house, which had fed on them. But the frogs, increasing tenfold, took up some of the slack as a food source.

These garter snakes, just twenty miles short of Canada, are blacker than the same species in southern Vermont because they need to absorb as much heat as possible during the brief summer season in order to digest what they eat; the sun is their engine. The woodchucks are blacker, too, not to accumulate heat but as camouflage: In these northern forests dark fur shows up less. The bears are black, the moose are black, the porcupines dark. The deer in their red summer coats look quite odd, as in fact they should because they followed the white men north.

In the house, I load the flashlights, put candles around, fill the kerosene lamps, and look to see if anything has been pilfered over the winter—pipe wrenches, a fire extinguisher, boots, blankets, or possibly my ax? Secondhand books sell hereabouts for a dollar a box, so no one steals books, though somebody once purloined the magnifying glass that went with my *Oxford English Dictionary*. And, once, my field glasses were lifted just before hunting season started, yet then were left on my woodpile during December. The next year, when it happened again, they weren't returned— this being such an impoverished area that woodpiles, too, are sometimes stolen. A furniture factory is the principal local employer, using the yellow birch and rock maple that people log around here when they aren't cutting pulpwood. Unemployment is so high it keeps wages low. Other people truck milk to Massachusetts, or cattle to the hamburger slaughterhouses down there. Where you see goshawks, red-tailed and broad-winged hawks, and peregrine falcons, you don't notice ads in the paper saying "Help Wanted."

My windows and rooms are small, as befits the cold climate most of the year. On some of the richest days, when a moose stalks by or a bear is blueberrying or munching hazelnuts outside, I think of my house as a bathysphere suspended in the wilderness. Nevertheless, it's comfortable— the floors painted russet, the furniture homey, the walls nearly covered with pictures I've taped up over the last quarter century. I'm partly surrounded by an eight-thousand-acre state forest, to which I'm leaving my land as a minor addition, except for the house, which will belong to my daughter. Big Valley Brook, Stillwater Swamp, May Pond, Boiling Spring, and Moose Mountain are spectacles that live in my head, yet I can walk to. If the weather muscles in, I chop four hours' worth of wood. I hear an owl; I hear the ravens; I hear a redstart.

Gardeners and trout fishermen got busy outdoors around mid-April this year, when the high water permitted; and the kids in town started shagging fungoes or fishing Kids' Brook, a stretch of stream near the fairgrounds so easy that it's lent to them. For me, spring had begun a month earlier, when a big male bobcat's tracks looped down off Moose Mountain into my wooded notch and intersected in a romancing scrawl with the solitary lady bobcat who shares the area with me. When the snow is gone, of course, her movements become more of a mystery, but my dog has treed her. On other rare occasions I notice her prints beside the pond or hear a rabbit scream at night, utterly suddenly, caught from ambush.

Then on the last day of March a bear that dens near my house left her little cave to enjoy what was perhaps her first drink in four months. Going a hundred feet so she could lap the trickling meltwater in a brook, her tracks showed that she made an immediate return trip to sleep some more. On Tax Day she was still in her den, her head protruding dozily, but the next day she descended a quarter mile to a patch of swamp to eat some cattails, with yearling-sized tracks accompanying her. The presence of the grown cub meant that, in the bearish biennial ritual, a male would probably come visit us in June so she could have new cubs next winter.

Among certain Indian tribes, a family used to inherit a given cluster of bear dens and the winter nutrition to be gained by killing the occupants in prudent rotation. Though I avail myself of the local supermarket, I'm just as protective: Don't mess with my bears. And the dog doesn't. Wally is a sheepdog and patrols the meadow aggressively but regards the forest as foreign territory. On the other hand, when the county airstrip comes to life and low-flying Cessnas angle over, he is inspired to defend the perimeter of our empty field from these roaring eagles with a pell-mell frenzy, as if we had a bevy of lambs that they might grab. Then after chasing a plane away, he'll cock his leg and pee triumphantly against a tree, the same as when his adversary has been a wandering fox or coyote, so it will know next time who it must reckon with.

He'll also mark a rabbit's trail, a squirrel's roost, a mouse's nest for later reference when he hunts, although I doubt he is one-tenth as efficient at that occupation as a fox. In June, I'll lie in the field at dusk and listen to a vixen's hectic rustle as she gleans a stomachful of meadow mice, deer mice, shrews, moles, night crawlers, and such to take back to her burrow and vomit for her pups. And I remember how quickly a woodchuck that had grown feisty from taunting Wally at the mouth of its hole fell prey to a lank coyote that rambled through. The coyote began to carry the body off, but stopped, dropped it, and performed an unexpected sort of victory dance, stiff-legged, around the corpse.

"Joy walking" is what deerhunters call what I do in the woods because I bring no gun. For Wally, as well, our outings are a matter of glee, not necessity. He'd rather simply sthan hunt for more than a few minutes himself. Carrion tastes, I suspect, a bit winy, cheesy, anchovy and green olivey, béarnaise and sour-creamy (which may be why we late primates try so hard to approximate the piquancy of fermentation with sauces). Wally drinks from muddy puddles and nibbles green sprouts as a further change from piped-in water and dog kibble before curling at my head as a sentinel when we camp out.

Wally celebrated spring around Tax Day by running down to the pond alone for his first swim: this when the wood frogs and song sparrows had just started to sing. I was lolling in a patch of sunny grass, watching a pair of robins, listening to a kinglet and a phoebe, but, lest my delight seem unadulterated, also picking off my first tick of the season. Instead of forest lore, Wally has become adept at reading human beings (hunters are the only predators he flees), such as the precise moment every morning when he can jump on my bed without waking and angering me—or the extraordinary value I place on the welfare of the goofy parrot in the kitchen, versus the crows in the garden, which he is encouraged to chase. They fly up into the basswood tree and razz him, then look for a hawk they can mob and mistreat.

HEADWORK

---◆---

M ore than a few people I know—the dairy farmer
down the road, the grocer in town who keeps me
fed, the gas deliveryman who brings propane—wonder how
I work, or maybe even what I do that's work, spinning stories out of my head. I have to dress more warmly than them
because my muscles aren't doing the job of working up a
sweat. Nor do I sell insurance or doctor people in a suit. I sit
up on my mountain road mostly alone, and yet they see me
go from the post office across to the bank from time to time,
and not with a check I have to cash, just something nice to
sock away. People they grew up with of course told stories
for free.

In my youth I worked hard physically for a while, fighting summer forest fires, trundling carts of tuna fish around
a cannery, setting up and tearing down a circus tent, buffing
floors on an army post. But by my twenties I began selling
words and memories and preferred to scrimp on living
expenses from then on and just do that. Later I took up
teaching to earn extra money, which can be great fun but is
a struggle occasionally—real work, when explaining to a

sleepy member of the MTV generation why Henry James still ought to count.

We say "real work" in referring to a demanding, exhausting, or wearisome job that perhaps we wouldn't do if we weren't being paid for the effort, or otherwise compelled. I'd never use the term when I am writing, for example, because I never write anything I wouldn't do for free if no one would employ me. I write to speak my mind, just as I sometimes teach for fun and would no doubt do that too, at least part-time, for no money if necessary.

"Real" work, therefore, is what I see other people do, like painting a house in the blazing sun, or hustling through an airport with two briefcases clutched in one hand to meet stacked-up business appointments and still catch the shuttle back that night. An optician grinding glasses, a lawyer fine-tuning a will, a production engineer with a clipboard, all have desks or work stations or whatever you want to call the place where they focus on the minutiae that make the world go round. One man's pleasant minutiae might be anathema to another, however. "God is in the details," we sometimes say. Or, conversely, "The Devil is in the details."

I need my glasses to shift adjectives around but wouldn't want to grind the lenses. Nor is it likely that the optician would enjoy spending an hour writing only a sentence or two, as I often do. I want my car to run, but not to *make* it run—much as the auto executive who pays one of my students' tuition may want her to experience Henry James without wishing to guide her through the lush terrain of James's prose himself. He speaks to her of the "real world" that awaits her after graduation, whereas naturally I think of superb novels as part of the real world and in all likelihood would regard some of the work he does after his daily commute as "real work," meaning what I wouldn't want to do.

In the sweat of thy face shalt thou eat bread, till thou return unto the ground; for out of it wast thou taken: for dust thou art, and unto dust shalt thou return, says my King James Version of God's covenant with Adam. And whether or not you are Christian, you have probably tasted sweat in your sandwiches many a noon. Though I don't sweat much now that I work indoors, even my dogs are disconcerted by how unable I am just to sit still, compose my thoughts, and organize my words. They like to stretch out beside my chair, but every time they settle themselves I'm up and pacing, or puttering into the next room, or out in the yard—yet fidget back to my typing table before they can get comfortable out there. Then after they've come inside to lie by me again, I'm up and going into the kitchen to bite a cracker, then outside to fill the bird feeder, till I hear the coffee water whistle, and back to type for two or three minutes, and so on. A friend asked whether I go to a gym, seeing that I'm a sixtyish type of slim. "No, I don't need to," I said. "I'm a writer."

The angst of students, not their obtusity, is what sometimes makes them difficult to teach. You're wrestling with shadows in their minds that you can't see. And it's hard work—once in a blue moon, "real work"—whereas in writing one is a true sovereign, the licensed master on the bridge. The shadows that one wrestles with are not somebody else's childhood traumas, for instance, but one's own and are less an obstruction than more grist for the mill. The rule of thumb I've learned to go by in commerce, "Trust almost everybody a little but almost nobody a lot," need not be consulted because one is solo.

And yet, as Robert Frost liked to say (perhaps because he was successful), "Everything must come to market." Even poems. As in other kinds of work, writers don't speak to just themselves; they must to some degree grip others. John Updike, when asked about posterity, responded that we can't know whose books posterity will find "useful." Did Jonathan Swift or Daniel Defoe imagine that two hundred and fifty years after their deaths we would be fans of theirs? Our job is to address strangers. My chair, my house, my car were designed and manufactured by people I won't ever lay eyes on. Nor will I see whoever reads this. No one but my dogs knows how frequently I jumped up in the midst of a paragraph, as my eyes itched from the hay outside and I nibbled pecans off an ancient piece of pie. And although my students do watch from a few feet away when I talk about Henry James or Henry Adams or Herman Melville, I doubt they realize that some of my best spiels are done simply by "winging it," free-associating about American literature from a lifetime of reading. Work, in other words, can become second nature, and you can't stop, don't want to stop, don't need to know who benefits—continuing with it for its own sake but with the destination of reaching other ears and minds, or a "trial by market," as Frost would say.

Though I haven't eaten a sandwich with proper sweat in it for years, I can ache from my neck to knees after a good day, and groan and fugue in front of the TV. My father was a lawyer in the city; and after I got old enough to drive, I'd meet his train in the evening and see how flat-out tired he was. He wrote the sort of corporate bonds that build oil refineries, so you might think it's a climb-down from him to me. And yet he envied me—supposed that what I did was Eden. I remember how badly I swung a sledgehammer in the circus in 1952, and how I usually brought up the rear with my Pulaski in chopping a fire line in 1953. I needed to live by my wits because I wasn't much good with my muscles.

"Work is a blessing. What would we do if we didn't work?" asks my neighbor, who operates a farm and seems to like his job as much as I like mine. You either find your work in life, or don't—like a mate, like stable health. It's as idiosyncratic, genetic, and mysterious as that. Without work, a person lives as if underwater, holding his breath, vaguely struggling. And grouchiness or neuroses may or may not stop you, because our productive lives are threaded through such a marbling of fat and waste anyway. We think with just a mote of our minds and act upon a tiny fraction of our impulses. The package of qualities that may lead to some success—showing up every day with a good-hearted or obsessive conscientiousness and a quick, intuitive take on other people—does not rule out all kinds of thorny, migrainey one-leggedness in other aspects of one's personality. People can be good fathers and bad breadwinners, or stymied in their love lives yet fine organizers and employees. I've sometimes felt on the verge of a breakdown but always managed to tiptoe back to the privacy of my house without going crazy publicly; and I'm sure that I'm not a rarity.

The gift of life can turn rancid if we press our luck and take too many chances, or seem as stale as a dead glass of beer if we risk nothing whatsoever. And this balance is perhaps epitomized in how we work: To "hold" a job, to please a readership, to keep a farm or business afloat year after year, shaking off the nutty spells and saving for a rainy day, yet making the most of the sunny ones.

EARTH'S EYE

———◆———

Water is our birthplace. We need and love it. In a bathtub, or by a lake or at the sea, we go to it for rest, refreshment, and solace. "I'm going to the water," people say when August comes and they crave a break. The sea is a democracy, so big it's free of access, often a bus or subway ride away, a meritocracy, sink or swim, and yet a swallower of grief because of its boundless scale—beyond the horizon, the home of icebergs, islands, whales. Tears alone are a mysterious, magisterial solvent that bring a smile, a softening of hard thoughts, lend us a merciful and inexpensive respite, almost like half an hour at the beach. In any landscape, in fact, a pond or creek catches and centers our attention as magnetically as if it were, in Thoreau's phrase, "earth's eye."

Lying on your back in deep meadow grass facing a bottomless sky is less focusing, but worth a drive of many hours, as weekend traffic will attest. Yet the very dimensions of the sky, which are unfathomable after the early surge of pleasure that they carry, cause most of us to mitigate their power with preoccupations such as golf or sunbathing as soon as we get outdoors. That sense of first principles can be unnerving, whereas the ground against our backs—if we lie gazing up into the starry night or a piebald day—is seething with groping roots and sprouting seeds, and feels like home, as the friendliest dappled clouds can't be. Beyond the prettiest azure blue is black, as nightfall will remind us, and when the day ends, cold is the temperature of black.

A pond, though, is a gentle spot (unless you are Ophelia). Amber or pewter-colored, it's a drinking fountain for scurrying raccoons and mincing deer, a water bugs' and minnows' arena for hunting insect larvae, a holding pen for rain that may coalesce into ocean waves next year. Mine flows into the St. Lawrence River. I live in Vermont and spent a hundred dollars once to bulldoze a tadpole pond next to my little stretch of stream. A silent great blue heron, as tall as a Christmas tree, and a castanet-rattling kingfisher, a faster flier and brighter blue, showed up to forage for amphibians the next year. Garter snakes also benefited from the occasional meal of a frog, and a red-tailed hawk, cruising by, might grab a snake or frog. More exciting, a bull moose began using it as a hot-weather wallow, soaking for half an hour, mouthing algae, munching sedges, and browsing on the willows that lean from the bank. A beaver cut down some poplar saplings to gnaw and stitch into a dam for creating a proper flow, but the depth remained insufficient to withstand a New England winter, so he retreated downstream to a wetland in my woods.

I bought this land for eighty-five dollars an acre in 1969, and today a comparable hideaway would probably still cost no more than about the price of a good car. We're not talking luxury: As with so much of life, your priorities are what count, and what you wish to protect and pay attention to. I've been a sinner in other ways, but not in this respect.

Remoteness bestows the amenity of uninterrupted sleep. No telephone or electric line runs by, and the hikers and pickups are gone by sunset. When the season of extravagant daylight shortens so I can't simply sleep from dusk to dawn, I light candles or kerosene, but in balmy weather I can nap with equal ease at any hour in the meadow too, or watch the swallows and dragonflies hawk after midges, as the breezes finger me and a yellowthroat hops in the bushes to eat a daddy longlegs. At dark the bats hawk for bugs instead, or an owl hunts, all wings, slow and mothlike, till it sees a rodent. The trees hang over a swimming hole nearby, with a dovish or a moonlit sky showing beyond the leaves like a kind of vastly enlarged swimming hole, until I feel I was born floating in both the water and the air. It's a hammock all the more beguiling because if you relax too much while swimming and let yourself sink, you might conceivably drown. Similarly, in the meadow, if you lazed too late into the fall, woolgathering, snow could fill your mouth.

Nature is not sentimental. The scenery that recruits our spirits in temperate weather may turn unforgiving in the winter. It doesn't care whether we love it and pay the property taxes to save it from development, having walked over it yard by yard in clement conditions. When the birds flee south and other creatures, from bears to beetles, have crawled underground to wait out the cold, we that remain have either got to fish or cut bait: burn some energy in those summer-lazy muscles cutting wood, or take some money out of the bank.

A mountain can be like that all at once. Summer at the bottom, winter at the top; and you climb through all the climates of the year as you scramble up. In the past half century I've climbed Mount Jefferson in Oregon (a cousin died there in a fall soon afterward), and Mount Washington in New Hampshire; Mount Katahdin in Maine, and Mount Etna in Sicily. I've clambered a bit in Wyoming's Wind Rivers and in the Absaroka Range; also in British Columbia and North Yemen; in the Western Ghats in southern India and the Alpes Maritimes in the south of France; and have scrambled modestly in the High Sierras, Alaska's Brooks Range, and on the lower slopes of Mount Kinyeti in the Imatong Massif in the southern Sudan. More particularly I climbed all of Vermont's firetower mountains, back when Vermont still used towers to locate fires, instead of planes.

This feast of variety is part of a writer's life, the coin of the realm you inhabit if you sacrifice the security Americans used to think they'd have if they weren't freelance in their working lives. In reality, everybody winds up being freelance, but mountains telescope the experience. During a weekend you climb from flowery summer glades to the tundra above tree line, slipping on patches of ice, trudging through snowdrifts; the rain turns to sleet. The view is rarefied until a bellying, bruise-colored sky turns formidable, not pretty. Like climbing combers in a strong surf, there's no indemnity if you come to grief. You labor upward not for money, but for joy, or to have *been somewhere*, closer to the mysteries, during your life. Finding a hidden alpine col, a bowl of fragile grassy beauty, you aren't just gleeful; you are linked differently.

Leaving aside specific dangers like riptides, vertigo, or terrific cold, I found I was comfortable on mountainsides or in seawater or in caves or wilderness swatches. In other words, I was fearful of danger but not of nature. I didn't harbor notions of any special dispensation, only that I too was part of it. I'd fought forest fires in the Santa Ana Mountains of southern California when I was twenty and had discovered that moderate hardship energized yet tempered me, as it does many people, just like the natural sorties for which one puts on hiking shoes and ventures where barefoot peoples used to go. In central Africa I've walked a little with tribesmen like the Acholi and the Didinga, who still tend to be comfortable when nearly naked, and have seen that the gap between us seems not of temperament or of intuitions, but only acculturation.

As virtual reality captures our time and obsessive attention, some of the pressures that are killing nature may begin to relent. Not the primary one of overpopulation, which is strangling the tropics; but as people peer more and more into computer screens and at television, the outdoors, in affluent countries, may be left in relative peace. This won't stop the wholesale extinction of species, the mauling of the ocean, or other tragedies, but close to home may give a respite to what's left of nature.

Where I live alone each summer, four families lived year-round eighty years ago. The other new landowners don't choose to occupy their holdings even in warm weather because of the absence of electricity. An unusual case, yet I think indicative, and supported by the recent return of numbers of adaptive sorts of wildlife, like moose and fisher, to New England—though, in contrast, along the lake a few miles downhill, cottages perch atop one another, motorboats and water-skiers buzz around, and trollers use radar fish-finders to trace the final sanctuaries of the schools that the lake still holds.

Just as habitat is the central factor in whether birds and animals can survive, what *we* are able to do in the woods will be determined by land regulation or taxing policy and public purchases. Maine's private timberlands have remained unpopulated because of America's lavish need for toilet paper—as Vermont's trees, too, make paper, cotton-mill bobbins, cedar fencing, and yellow-birch or maple dowels that become furniture legs. Any day, I watch truckloads of pulpwood go by. And in the California Sierras above Lake Tahoe, or on the pristine sea island of Ossabaw, off Savannah, Georgia, I've devoted lovely, utterly timeless hours to exploring refuges that seem quite empty of people, but are actually allotted in careful fashion by state or federal agencies for intensive recreational use. The animals hide while the sun is up and feed when it's down. This is the way it will have to work. Levels of life on the same acreage. Or else it won't work at all.

I can be as jubilant indoors, listening to Schubert or Scott Joplin, as when sauntering underneath a mackerel sky on a day striped yellow, red, and green. Indeed, the density of sensations in which we live is such that one can do both—enjoy a virtuoso pianist through a headset outside. We live two lives or more in one nowadays, with our scads of travel, absurd excesses of unread informational material, the barrage of Internet and TV screens, wallpaper-music, the serializing of polygamy and the elongation of youth blurring old age. A sort of mental gridlock sometimes blocks out the amber pond, the mackerel sky, the seething leaves in a fresh breeze up in a canopy of trees, and the Walkman's lavish outpouring of genius, too. Even when we just go for a walk, the data jams.

Verisimilitude, on computer screens or in pictorial simulation, is carrying us we don't entirely know where. I need my months each year without electricity and a telephone, living by the sun and looking down the hill a hundred times a day at the little pond. The toads sing passionately when breeding, observing a hiatus only at midmorning when the moose descends from the woods for his therapeutic wallow, or when a heron sails in for a meal. I see these things so clearly I think our ears have possibly changed more than our eyes under the impact of civilization—both the level of noise and subtleties of sound are so different from hunter-gatherer whisperings. I'm a worrier, if not a Luddite. The gluttonies that are devouring nature are remorseless, and the imbalances within the human family give me vertigo. The lovely old idea that human life is sacred, each soul immortal, is in the throes of a grand mal seizure; overpopulation is doing it in. I didn't believe that, anyway, but did adhere to the transcendental idea that heaven is right here on earth, if we perceive and insist on it. And this faith is also becoming harder to sustain.

"Religion is what the individual does with his own solitariness," as A. N. Whitehead said. ("Thus religion is solitariness; and if you are never solitary, you are never religious," he added.) I fall back on elemental pleasures like my love of ponds, or how my first sight of any river invariably leaves me grinning. And the sheen of rainwater on a bare, black field in March. The thump of surf, combed in the wind and foaming, glistening, yet humping up again like a dinosaur. Yet fish don't touch me as much as animals, perhaps because they never leave the water. Frogs *do*; and I seem to like frog songs even more than bird songs, maybe because they're two-legged like us but can't fly either and were the first vertebrate singers. But I especially respond to them because they live a good deal more than we do in the water.

Frogs are disappearing worldwide in a drastic fashion, perhaps because of ultraviolet rays or acid rain; and I may finally cease to believe that heaven is on earth, if they do. Water without dolphins, frogs, pelicans, cormorants will not mean much to me. But in the meantime I like to search out springs in the high woods where brooks begin—a shallow sink in the ground, perpetually filling. If you carefully lift away the bottom covering of waterlogged leaves, you'll see the penny-sized or pencil-point sources of the groundwater welling up, where it all originates—the brook, the pond, the stream, the lake, the river and the ocean, till rain brings it back again.

I HAVE SEEN
THE ELEPHANT

Towns exist north of the Arctic Circle, and not just pre-fabricated white-men's towns; the Arctic has been inhabited for many thousands of years. But Antarctica is different. Individual people couldn't set foot and begin to survive there until the early nineteenth century, when they had sophisticated means to sail away immediately again. Besides, Antarctica is a mountainous continent that is believed to have sheared off of Australia as much as eighty-five million years ago, instead of a gigantic cap of ice that sits atop an ocean, as the core of the Arctic is; and there-fore Antarctica manufactures its own gelid, horrendous weather, insulated by hundreds of miles of pitching ocean on all sides, instead of borrowing the climate patterns of neighboring continents and blending and chilling them, as the Arctic does. And Antarctica has no land mammals, no caribou, moose, musk oxen, polar bears, grizzlies, white wolves, hares, lemmings, foxes, as large regions above the Arctic Circle do. Only sea creatures make fitful visits to its margins (how *would* an Eskimo have lived there?), which makes its sometimes tumultuous landscape seem even starker in the mind's eye than the Arctic's pale terrain.

To get to Antarctica, you fly south from Miami for eight hours over the length of South America to the international city of Buenos Aires. Then you fly on again for four or five more hours, over the pampas and over Patagonia, and the strait discovered by Ferdinand Magellan in 1520, to Tierra del Fuego, and finally land in the windy frontier settlement of Ushuaia ("Ooshwhy-a"), Argentina's southernmost, which fronts Charles Darwin's fabled Beagle Channel. The little cruise ships that briefly flirt with the Antarctic Peninsula (the "banana belt" of Antarctica), whose northern tip still lies seven hundred miles away, beyond Cape Horn and across stormy Drake Passage, between the Atlantic and Pacific—which Sir Francis Drake blundered upon fifty-eight years after Magellan's tamer discovery—tie up here.

Mine was a stubby, two-thousand-ton, thirty-eight-passenger, ice-hardened Russian research vessel, the *Professor Molchanov*. The professor had been a distinguished Soviet atmospheric scientist who was murdered by Stalin's NKVD during the Nazi siege of Leningrad but whose reputation was later "rehabilitated"; and it is characteristic that the Russian government, now desperate for dollars, is converting even their arctic-weather ships to carry bevies of American trippers to the Antarctic, and that the few other passengers on the *Professor Molchanov* were Germans: like the Russians, a recently defeated people whose principal task dictated by the victors was that they learn English. The *Professor Molchanov* had been leased by two entrepreneurs in Connecticut and then re-leased by them to a retailing outfit, Mountain Travel, with offices near Berkeley, California, which had provisioned it in Hamburg, Germany. It was half empty, however, because of competition from the *Vavolov*, a bigger sister ship, and the *Kapitan Khlebuikov*, equipped with survey helicopters, as well as the four-hundred-passenger *Marco Polo* (formerly the *Alexander Pushkin*), the two-hundred-and-fifty-passenger *Bremen*, the St. Louis–owned *Discoverer*, the New York–owned *Explorer*, the New Zealand–owned *Asiatic*, and so on. A new destination creates a scramble.

Ushuaia, surrounded by snowy, stunted mountains, and a low timberline, resembles an Alaskan coastal town, with its hasty housing, higgledy-piggledy storefronts, and thrown-up hoardings, the off-road three-wheelers sharing the sparse streets with regular autos, the malamute prints hardened into a stretch of sidewalk paving, and the varied, occasionally Indian-looking faces. Two huge Japanese drift-net trawlers, the *Kongo* and the *Yamato*, were tied up along the single wharf, opposite the *Bremen* and my *Professor Molchanov*. This had been a convict town, and Tierra del Fuego was Argentina's Siberia, after the Yahgans, the indige-nous people who hollered so vigorously at Darwin and at Robert Fitzroy, the captain of the *Beagle* in that winter of 1832–33, succumbed to European diseases, rifles, liquor, and whatnot. (Their signal fires gave Tierra del Fuego its name.) Then Ushuaia somewhat resumed its role as a prison colony during the terrible years of the junta in the 1970s, when political prisoners, if they were lucky, were exiled here. But mainly the population is descended from nearly two centuries' worth of sailors, stowaways, and other human flotsam who jumped ship or were jettisoned by their skip-pers in rounding Cape Horn, such as you will see washed up in other end-of-the-world ports. The "Roaring Forties" and "Screaming Fifties" these extreme latitudes were called—

though you don't reach the Antarctic Circle itself until you're at sixty-six and one-half degrees south—and surviving them at all in a sailing ship was surely enough of a pedigree to hoist a beer here.

Wind shear, in this nervous, penultimate climate, made the short, gusty airstrip a bit hairy. In town, I went to Tante Elvira's, a restaurant in a gray shack on the main street that I'd heard about from a friend who lives in Topeka, Kansas, and enjoyed crab bisque, sourdough bread, and three-cheese "butter," sitting next to two local nuns, who couldn't persuade the proprietor to take their money. I got on the ship with the pilot, who was saturnine, wiry, grizzled-haired, his English resembling the sort of a seafaring Spaniard who is posted next to Gibraltar. Chile and Argentina had recently been squabbling over these scant, cold archipelagos to such a breaking point that the Pope in Rome needed to be brought in to mediate a compromise. Looking across the Beagle Channel at Navarino Island, which belongs to Chile, and at a Chilean gunboat prowling by, the pilot ventured a joke about the military mind—his own nation's as well as theirs.

Our skipper, Gennadiy Nikitin, was a young thirty-nine, both agile and stooped in his posture, rather gentle-faced, wearing jeans and a sweater, and shyly friendly to the passengers. At first the mates and helmsman had seemed more officious. "I'm Gennadiy," he said, and told me he'd served as a bridge officer on an auxiliary frigate in the Soviet fleet before transferring to civilian ships like the *Professor Molchanov*. "On the little boats in the navy they didn't notice me as much, so it was easier to leave."

The whipsaw winds, the piebald sky deepening to a red sunset, the choppy mountains separated by blunt dogleg valleys, all had a provisional quality, as though a bouncing gale or a summer snowstorm or blind-man's fog could blow in from any direction while you weren't looking. Navarino Island, which is even more sparsely populated than Tierra del Fuego, conveyed the same brink-of-the-world severity, rolling from its shingle beaches up toward an interior that you knew was quite shallow, before the melodramas of the Southern Ocean began.

The Yahgans had built dozens of bonfires along Beagle Channel, so I peopled the narrow beaches and brushy cliffs and darkish coves that we were passing, once we'd cast off, with these. The Yahgans had been a naked, canoeing people, estimated at six thousand, and are reckoned to have been among the most primitive people on earth when Darwin, then twenty-three, saw them—far inferior to Eskimos, for example, in their level of craftsmanship. They fought by throwing stones, never having invented spears or bows; didn't know how to thatch a hut for shelter from the year-round storms, living instead in flimsy grass "wigwams"; and had no priests, chiefs, or artisans: in fact, no word for the concept of "God," though a missionary did record a Yahgan language totaling over thirty thousand words. They were preyed upon by a local forest tribe, called the Onas, who were larger in stature, used better weapons, built better housing, painted themselves, and—though the Onas never ventured out onto the water—at least by wearing guanaco skins on their bodies and as hats and shoes, had invented clothes.

Standing next to me on Gennadiy's bridge was a house-wife in her late fifties, married to a chemical engineer for Clorox, who said that she was making this trip partly in memory of her father, a naval architect who had designed engine rooms and had always wanted to see the White Continent himself. Another woman, late forties, was a bank vice president, single, with a doctorate in American history. She wanted to experience Antarctica as the exemplar of solitude, "the best substitute for voyaging in space." And there was a widower, a power-company president from Iowa who was wetting his feet in the new world of recreational adventure for the first time, as we steamed eastward down Darwin's channel. He was an exception to the rule that Antarctica visitors are sophisticates who have not only already been to Paris and Venice, but have rafted and trekked in Papua New Guinea and Bhutan. (The banker had toured Vietnam on her own last year.) When I asked, "Why Antarctica?" he said his friends at the Rotary Club had asked him the same. "I'll tell you later, when I've seen it," he said rather tentatively, because his wife of forty years was dead and he wasn't convinced yet about any of the choices he was trying to make.

Our ironic pilot's job was negotiating dryly with the various Chilean and Argentinean gunboats we passed, and with the Chilean navy base at Puerto William, as much as calibrating our route. We saw very few lights, so I could fantasize that the Yahgans, southernmost humans in the world, still lurked along shore. Perforce a littoral people, they lived in fear of the woodsy, valley-dwelling Onas on the Tierra del Fuego side, but when a European castaway floated off a shipwreck, they toyed with and tortured him; might burn and eat him. Aiming for the eyes, they were terrific stone throwers, if landing parties tried to rescue him, but ordinarily lived on mussels, birds, turtles, birds' eggs, turtles' eggs. They hunted seals with clubs or ate dead creatures that washed up on the beach, and fished with lines that the women plaited from their own hair. I scanned the steeply darkening, grass-topped mountains, imagining signal fires and hollers that would be exasperating and barbaric, if you had reason to be afraid of them.

We saw the tiny lights of several sheep stations and dropped the pilot near Picton Island—"Five people and a quarter million sheep," he said. I then slept a few hours, till at around two-thirty the dawn began to finger a low band of the sky with apricot and peach colors, when we were some miles off the Gibraltar-like bulk of Cape Horn—which is itself an island, longish and high-ended.

The seas now flexed in a whimsical, hard-slamming rumpus like Goliath on a binge, unimpeded by any mass of land separating the two oceans that ran east and west around the globe. The horizon tilted precipitously, and we experienced double gravity in alternation with weightlessness every twelve or thirteen seconds. The floor kept rising under my feet and tipping me back into my bunk, or altering the position of my pant legs as I tried to get dressed. The purple sea turned glinty gray, pitching us about like a double-jointed seesaw, an unhinged carousel.

"Rock and roll," Chuck Cross, our expedition leader, called it. And Greg Myer, our birding guide, who was from California, said that the rough handling we would get from this Drake Passage across the fabled Southern Ocean was how we'd "earn Antarctica." Sometimes tourists complain that they can't just fly from Tierra del Fuego and skip the nausea of the Screaming Fifties, but another of our "lecturers"—as these young chip-on-the-shoulder escorts who accompany trippers to far-flung spots are called—was a spirited Brazilian, Suzana d'Oliveira, and she said she had watched as twenty-two of "her" tourists died in a crash at Puerto William, the short Chilean airstrip, like Ushuaia's, on the Beagle Channel. Their charter plane couldn't stop on the tarmac and slid into the water like a rocking horse. At the front, the food cart blocked one exit and an emergency chute at the rear inflated too soon and blocked the other. She'd flown in on the first trip, "with the baggage and the Germans," and, being a vigorous, resourceful woman, she ran, swam, and climbed up onto the wing and pounded at the chute even as the passengers were drowning inside.

(The father of a friend of mine, as I learned later, happened to be on that plane, and survived by quickly making for the rear when he saw the fatal food cart, and dragged his wife and several others out before the chute inflated. Once outside, while they were babbling in relief, he discovered that he had already saved the life of one of these strangers before. They'd been shipmates on a subchaser that had sunk in a typhoon off Ulithi Isle in the Yap Island chain before the invasion of Iwo Jima in 1945.)

The seas swung like five pendulums at cross-purposes; and, fighting the floor, which lifted and fell away right when I'd calculated that it might plan to stay where it was, I conceived a particular love for my bed. It was a day to lose a pound. Seasickness knocked the jet lag out of me like pneumonia supplanting a common cold. From the poop deck I watched giant petrels kiting in the wind and a wandering albatross sailing tirelessly with locked wings. An hourglass dolphin porpoised through the water and two rockhopper penguins were doing the same. I remembered my first intercontinental sea voyage from Manhattan to Lisbon and Palermo, on my honeymoon in 1960.

The ship creaked. The Russian crew, ice hardened, was from Murmansk, though Sergey, the sallow-skinned radioman, was Belarussian in ethnicity, and Dalî, the bartender, was Georgian—a very angry Georgian because she'd been at home visiting her family during the bitter fighting four months before in Sukhumi. Shells had hit her house, her brother was killed in the battle, and Dalî ran through forests and brambles to save her life, collecting bruises that she could show me still. Their wages were microscopic, ranging from six dollars a day for an able-bodied seaman to sixteen dollars for our excellent captain, and so by the end of the voyage we travelers were giving away everything we thought that we could—in my case, my boots, raincoat, hat, shirts, and socks. I teased Gennadiy that the *Professor Molchanov* was togged out like a spy ship because of the electronics with which it did research when not ferrying rich Americans. He'd hung off Cuba and Cape Canaveral on real spy ships, but had never landed on American soil. His complexity pleased me—a democrat whose father had spent twenty-three years in Siberia for political incorrectness but who, when talk turned to rebuilding the new Russia, quoted Genghis Khan. Like the rest of the crew, he despised both Mikhail Gorbachev and Boris Yeltsin. War was inevitable; there would always be war; Gorbachev hadn't forestalled the threat of war, Gennadiy said.

We travel partly to define ourselves and flesh out who we are, or else perhaps to try to fulfill an authentic passion (icebergs, flamenco, Alfred Sisley, whatever it is)—or to heal a central puzzlement, a grief, or a defeat, bursting a chrysalis that has held us back so we can begin anew. This is ambitious, exhausting travel, after a divorce or death, but other people travel to try to shore up their sense of domesticity, seeking a frisson of physical danger to reassure themselves that they're still spry, while amassing a secret store of shimmering memories to draw upon when immersed back home. Still others simply want to sound more interesting when asked where they've been.

The Drake Passage was stern medicine, hard too on the crew and the ship, which, under their present charter arrangements, shuttled continually back and forth across it every two weeks every year from November to April. We shuddered as if the ship were an old saddle bronco, as used to the jarring, stiff-legged hullabaloo of a rodeo as any wrangler. The hours progressively seemed to lower my braincase down onto the back of my eyeballs and the roof of my mouth and herniated my stomach into a sore, sour knot. The waves were like an out-of-sync trampoline, but then amidst coruscating sunshine, two finback whales emerged like sudden embolisms, utter masters of that same rhythm, as they rolled, breached, and blew. Much in the way we don't swallow at the same time as we take a breath, the whales effortlessly factored every unsynchronous heave into the tempo of their spouts. The spray thrown up by our bow created falling rainbows.

I was glad to sleep in bouts of a couple of hours so as to miss less, going up on deck in between. My dreams, however, were scary ones, as if to acknowledge that we were on our way to the White Continent. Yet they weren't about the tides or ice—no foundering ship and sleety, sloshing lifeboats under the lee of a titanic iceberg. Instead they went back to my late adolescence and the circus tigers I had cared for as part of a summer job. Hip-high and pungent, they stalked the floor so close to me that their bristling whiskers brushed my arm; the hair in the small of my back was electrified. Then, abruptly, in the way dreams have, a surreal telescoping of forty years occurred, to the corrosive, poignant, heart-palpitating death of my quarter-century marriage and, later, my wife's losing struggle with cancer, whose final stages I nevertheless witnessed from beside her bed. Not *all* of this, of course, but a swift unnerving silhouette of her in anger, ill health, and distress that packed a wallop and sent me up to walk the deck. I'd had a recent siege of semi-blindness myself, and my surgeon had told me after operating that I should see whatever I wanted to of the world before my difficulties recurred. So here I was, gorging my eyes on the slanting, kiting birds, the flux of black geometric waves in endless mad triangles, and the first drifting icebergs—absurdist cubes, sliced with a cake knife and white as snow—cruising the Southern Ocean (benign-sounding name!), where the Indian, Atlantic, and Pacific oceans converge, shrapneling storms with a clockwise spin: but not really concerned about a maritime disaster or any considered action of my own, just my inner baggage.

When on the open deck, I treated the rail in the rather affectionate, gingerly manner I'd perfected for tigers, staying a little bit out of reach, admiring the glistering sea without leaning right over the maw of the rushing waves. Ever since I was fifteen and went on a voyage with my father from Bayonne, New Jersey, to Galveston, Texas, on an Esso oil tanker, I've had a kind of "secret sharer" who wants to slide inconspicuously over the side of a ship, or the edge of a cliff. Unlike in Joseph Conrad's novel, he never does, so I've never been rid of him. An overriding impulse sustained for just a moment might do it, and in Antarctic waters, the act would be irreversible. You couldn't bob up to wave an arm and shout, "Throw me a line"—though I *would* change my mind. Thus I moved along toward the enclosed bridge lightly like a spectator, not hypnotized like the proverbial bird drawn to a snake. I was bored by my handicap and had survived and enjoyed two weeks on the Bering Sea not many years before, where the absurd narcissism and blind solipsism of a frivolous act of suicide would also have been thrown into relief: self-destruction in the midst of prehistoric, vaulting grandeur. But I was on this trip for keeps. If my mind skidded out of kilter in the next fortnight, there wasn't any sanatorium to check into, only the vertigo of the bucking wind, the slamming sea, the cryptic sky, the haunting grisly icebergs jostling one another in a slot between colliding banks of fog. And my mouth tasted of vomit, not majesty.

But I loved the pretty, flickering, brown-and-white, almost-speckled birds known as pintado petrels that materialized alongside us in numbers by the second day, swooping at the krill our ship turned up. Also blue and Wilson's storm petrels, and prions, fulmars, and black-browed albatrosses, lofting me with a jiggling gaiety, a certainty that I was in the right place. So often, indeed, there's a disjunction between the sights one sees and the taste in one's mouth: unutterable beauty to gorge upon, and yet seasickness; or, at the other extreme, a delicious meal in a scrumptious restaurant, when you're sitting across the table from people who are both miserable and dislikable. In the shaving mirror in my cabin, I was startled to discover that I had turned white-haired since my last ocean voyage, which had been on the *Discoverer* out of Nome. Exhaustion, nausea, dysentery, an unshakable cough, or a lady-or-the-tiger sense of imminent possibilities have gone with more than a few of my richer experiences, so it seemed natural to tiptoe alongside the shuddering rail, while en route to the one polar continent.

Wham-bam waves splashed over the bow, spraying the bridge windows dramatically. We had a two-hundred-degree, glassed-in view, and a cherrywood table with drawers full of

Soviet and British Admiralty charts to pore over, plus the round radar scope that when peered into looked like a planetarium ceiling on which new icebergs began showing up like spatterings of stars. We heard occasional "growlers"—chunks of floating pack ice—scrape noisily along our hull, and saw "bergy bits," the next size up, which might stand a dozen feet out of the water, not heroic statuary like the genuine "tabular" icebergs. Flat walled, flat topped, and about a hundred feet high, these monumental constructions, sometimes castellated or jaggedly eroded or gigantically cubic, had calved off the Larsen Ice Shelf, hundreds of miles away in the Weddell Sea. We encountered them as we got within fifty miles of the first of the South Shetland Islands.

For ten or fifteen hours we sailed past spellbinding flotillas—dozens, and then more dozens. Big as a building, or a city block, or an entire neighborhood, each specimen was cut slightly differently, unevenly white with granular seams of blue or platinum, and a few had flipped over during a storm and been scrubbed at, top and bottom, by the waves. They were rounded, creased, shelved, and their patina of immaculate white had been stained with ancient interior dirt that had melted out. Their surfaces were marred by protuberances, tin-colored, lead-colored, which lent them an aura of mortality. Though hard as concrete, they weren't frozen cubes, unearthly and uncompromising. They were now *aging* and could start to sing to our intuitions.

The Arctic, too, proffers this lavish plethora of white, but the Arctic has been inhabited for millennia and is a country of myth and mysticism, anthropomorphic gods and mammalian dangers, whereas Antarctica boasts a tumultuous landscape where even moss and lichens are barely present, and seabirds and sea creatures make only fitful visits. The lore is instead top-heavy with the feats of breast-beating European explorers. So you have something different—on the order of another planet—where penguins arrive as from a spaceship every November to land on certain ice-bare beaches for egg-laying. Yet twenty-six nations have established fifty research stations for human occupancy, laying claim to zones of influence, should the continent's mineral resources be opened to exploitation.

We were now well inside the winter rim of the pack ice, which waxes and wanes hundreds of miles every year, and thus sailing on borrowed time. Perhaps because I'm a professor myself, my thoughts kept straying to our namesake professor, Molchanov, who had been shot in the head by one of his police guards as he lay in shackles in the snow on frozen Lake Ladoga, outside Leningrad. I couldn't reconstruct how weakened by hunger and beatings he may have been, or whether he had been arrested in a general roundup of intellectuals or targeted because he was a scientist of repute who had attended international conferences, amassed a file of correspondence with colleagues in other countries, and participated with them in some of the pioneering weather flights of the German dirigible *Graf Zeppelin.*

"He was shotten. He got died," Gennadiy said, remembering his own father's tale of a forced march from the Ural Mountains, where their family had been rich landowners, to northwestern Siberia as a boy of eleven, accompanied by his grandmother. In his years in Arctic Siberia, he had become a construction supervisor of such acumen that he won permission to move to Murmansk and build shipyards there, where he married. Gennadiy, born after World War II, enrolled in the Naval Academy at age seventeen and after eight years of service off Africa and America transferred to nonmilitary duty. He was a quick study at learning English—as he must have been at maritime science to become a captain so soon—and later he asked if I would help him translate a family memoir he was writing. His mother lived in a three-room cabin on a dab of their old property in the Urals, where, unmarried, he spent his leaves. Unassuming, although his bashfulness was a form of civility with these American guests, he told me that a psychological "sickness" had overwhelmed the Russian people. Even the educated ones were reading trash to distract themselves from the collapse of their country and "bury their heads in the sand." He himself was happier at the ends of the earth, meeting Americans, seeing the terrain, and reading the Russian classics in his cabin, though he didn't yet know Nabokov and said that he thought writers like Pasternak and Solzhenitsyn were "too angry." His gently gloved comments reminded me of a favorite teacher I had had, but then he'd startle me with a conquistador quotation from Alexander the Great, or a remark about women, when I asked if he was married: "Women are like a ship," he said. "They may look different, but they all work the same."

Two mornings south of Cape Horn, using the inflatable rubber, outboard-driven minicraft known as Zodiacs, we landed on a little shingly ironstone beach on a steep slope of Joinville Island, a tip of the submerged Andes just off the Antarctic Peninsula. Bouldery gravel from higher up lay on the remnant ice just above us, with cleaner swatches of bright white snow left by the miniature slides that had occurred in the summer thaw. A small colony of gentoo penguins was nesting here, several hundred creating a steady racket of cries, which were mostly unrelated to us. They were jockeying with and encouraging one another, yet the space that they had, bare of snow, was so very limited they seemed terribly vulnerable. Gentoos are the "mellowest" species of penguins, Greg Myer said, and though obviously uneasy they were not panicked by the arrival of twenty human beings on their tiny beach. Penguins' predators are leopard seals and killer whales, which hunt them in the deep, and ravenlike birds called skuas that cruise overhead to steal their eggs or seize their chicks when they are ashore. So they have no instinctive fear of an apparition approaching on foot during this relatively short period of the year when they are beached.

I sat down in the cheek-by-jowl congestion on this sparse scoop of stones and sand. In fact, I disapproved of our being on Joinville Island at all, now that I was here. It was too small for the penguins to be subjected to a crowd of people—we had all the rest of the world. Yet I was excited to be thrust among my first penguins in Antarctica, as if thousands of preceding millennia hadn't yet happened. The island rattled with subsurface meltwater and diverse rocky trickles and a spindly waterfall. Where moisture sheltered minute growths of moss, it was faintly green, but mostly the slopes were dirty white, cut by rust-colored outcroppings or scree. By the penguins' roosts you could see lightish red stains in the snow from the krill in the birds' guano. Krill are the inch-long crustaceans that during the sun-shot January summer grow in extraordinary masses underwater, weighing as much as thirty pounds per cubic yard.

My pity for the penguins was not based on there being a great shortage of them. The massacre of most of the world's krill-eating whales has been a boon to penguins because of the new abundance of food. Nor does Antarctica present a shortage of beaches in this brief window of weeks when they can hatch their eggs and nurture their chicks. The beaches are few but Antarctica is big, so there are extra beaches. The chicks were pretty large by now, January 17—astir and standing up, although still fuzzy and an infantile brownish silvery gray. The parents, besides the vociferous gabbly quarreling they did over nest pebbles with neighboring pairs— pebbles are the only nesting material and serve as anchors or markers too—and their clamorous high yodeling with red bills pointed skyward (known to scientists as "ecstatic display"), were also engaged in the long grind of waddling down to the water and uphill again, fetching food in their crops. Penguins can't fly and aren't made for walking, so it's touching to watch them struggle along in their pelagic camouflage. The dynamics are unforgiving because a colony must achieve a sort of critical mass to succeed. It must be densely populated for the chicks to survive the skuas' sneaky hawklike dives from different angles out of the sky. The outer ring of nests suffers plenty of losses anyway. Yet if the colony is large and crowded enough to mostly foil the gathering skuas, the adult penguins must swim farther and farther out from shore to capture their share of food, then climb the slope laboriously again when they return. And because leopard seals wait for them in the waves, some never do come back. The second parent, waiting at the nest for its turn to eat, eventually must leave if it is not to starve, and the skuas swoop and tear at the single chick left behind, while other parents merely mind their own offspring.

High is certainly tougher, as you watch the penguins climb from the beach by an endless progression of clumsy hops to reach the lofty site of their special niche. Because of the work of the trip, it might be assumed that the youngest, least experienced parents have been pecked and shouldered out from below and forced to settle for space high up. But, on the contrary, the huskier, wiser-looking old birds—some of the strongest—pitch their nests on a particular ledge to catch more of the early-warming and earlier-in-the-season sun. Toiling up and down all day and swimming out to chance the leopard seals, they do their utmost until, like all the other parent penguins, they finally get played out and swim way off for an extended respite in the ocean to regain their strength. The abandoned young, meanwhile, waiting to finish growing thermal feathers and sufficient musculature to face the sea, cluster and lean into each other in what ornithologists, in an inspired bit of nomenclature, call "creches," for safety in numbers against the piratical skuas. Together, eventually they take the perilous plunge, and the leopard seals, lurking in the wings for these tyro swimmers, enjoy their biggest feast of the year.

I knew some book biology, but as I sat on the rocks trying to ignore the fact that twenty other tourists around me were in search of a vaguely similar epiphany, I was reaching for a concordance with penguin time, ocean time, and weather time, which is not digitalized like ours but instead goes in surges. Subsistence cultures live in surges too—sleep, eat, and exert themselves in what we might define as whims and binges—not pacing themselves with a metronome as we do. In seeking what the biologist E. O. Wilson has called "deep history," we fugue back however far we can, one hundred or one thousand years, from clockwork timing to something a little like surge time. Hard to do. I can accomplish it for ten or twenty minutes if I try.

One of my fellow passengers had endeared himself to me on the first day—on the airport bus in Buenos Aires—by taking off his tramping hat to show me how his dog drank out of it on their hiking trips in Colorado. He was a retired officer type and track coach who ran marathons, climbed mountains, and ran up Pike's Peak annually; indeed he had won an Olympic bronze medal as a young man, I learned later, and not from him. Geeky and scoutmasterly in a way that my writing had mostly saved me from, he therefore seemed an alter ego.

There was also a retired political science professor from Michigan: matter-of-fact, quizzical, decent, and a string bean, well up on his reading. And a fiftyish woman in the video business, with what she said were marital problems, and a somewhat anxious, haunting face, whose passion for beauty and adventure warred with her vulnerability to sea-sickness and other frailties. Also a likable young securities lawyer from Toronto, not yet formed or crystallized by marriage, as you had the sense he'd soon be. And a couple of travel agents from San Diego, husband and wife. The husband's tangled head of hair and fiercely bushy, jutting beard looked more like a sea captain's than any real sea captain's I've ever known. And a corrections psychotherapist from the Rockies with an extraordinarily sensitive face who read airport novels on the bridge as we passed much of the best Antarctic scenery. He reminded me a bit of the travel agent who looked more like a sea dog than the captain did, because of his misleadingly sensitive face, which turned out to be an expression of the travails childhood polio had inflicted on him. And a German engineer who worked for the Bayer Company in Cologne and told me he had visited sixty countries in eleven years of off-time rambling. Also a sales clerk from Chicago who had just lost her job and con-sequently had money worries, but talked most often of the great love of her life, who had flown over the Hump in the Himalayas during World War II (it turned out that our retired professor had been a landing officer at an airfield there), and was in frank search of a revelation on this journey, such as the organizers of this cruise had already facilitated for her in rafting trips down the Bíobío in Chile and the Tatshenshini in southeast Alaska. She was soon my favorite chum, along with the Toronto lawyer, the video woman, the professor, and a youngish Tasmanian environmentalist who was studying our "impact."

Mountain Travel, which began business in the San Francisco area twenty-five years ago by taking paying clients to the heights of Nepal, regards itself as the granddaddy of adventure companies, though I liked to tease them by saying that they were really just New Age White Hunters because of the spiritual spin that they attempt to instill on their trips. They were Ernest Hemingway and we were Francis Macomber. But Lynn Cross, director of their polar operations and our official escort, whose husband, Chuck, was our expedition leader, wasn't convinced. A professor's daughter from Illinois, she had gone to bartending school after graduating from college and spent the next seven years in the bar business before getting thoroughly tired of talking with people "who could never remember the next day what they'd said" and gravitating into travel as a livelihood. Now forty, she still had a wiry, waiflike look, like so many of the women who labor over the books in the back rooms of bars, emerging now and then into the Antarctica of drunks and misanthropes and ne'er-do-wells with a shyly maternal or authoritative smile, and she had retained that patient, slightly pedantic manner in handling tourists that works so well with saloon buffoons and barflies and was also vaguely

reminiscent of her college major, early childhood studies—
staring persuasively at people who didn't at first cooperate.

Chuck was fifty-two, his marriage to Lynn recent, and it
appeared to be a complementary one. Chuck was chunky,
his beard and hair a mix of black and gray, and rather bleak
of face except where his thick eyeglasses managed to mag-
nify his eyes enough to show their inner vulnerability. A
mountaineer with what he summed up as "twenty years of
climbing and then twenty years of skiing" behind him, he
lurched when he walked as if the level ground were not his
native milieu and he were attempting to push off from it.
Chuck's reserve was such that I couldn't inquire whether,
like many climbers I have known, he had been markedly
singed at some point and climbed to get *up, up and away.*
But he did tell me, rocking on his feet, that lately he was
growing more content to gaze at a height of land without
immediately beginning to scheme how he could get himself
on top of it. He seethed with a scrambler's energy. His
proudest possession was a racing sailboat in San Francisco
Bay, and as a youngster he had climbed Mount Rainier
twenty-five times by twelve different routes, under the influence of a charismatic English teacher at Oregon State who
later died on an icefall on Mount Everest. Chuck was enthusiastic about the ocean but his stomach wasn't. He was a
landsman and there was a sort of reverse-pole electricity to
his movements, which seamen, even the restless ones, seldom show. Engaged in a commercial enterprise, they make
their living by accommodating themselves to the tides of
nature—not by conquest, like a mountain climber, who
probably earns his living elsewhere.

Mountain Travel Company has a "Grand Slam" program
for escorting Francis Macombers up the highest summits on

every continent in the world. They count seven: Kilimanjaro (19,321 feet) in Africa; Aconcagua (22,834 feet) in South America; Djaja (16,500 feet) in New Guinea, which is classed as Oceania; Vinson (16,850 feet) in Antarctica; and of course Mounts McKinley (20,323 feet) and Everest (29,028 feet). Mad, spiky, frenetic millionaires could add Kosciusko, in Australia, and Kinabalu, in Borneo. Chuck himself had climbed two of these, and wore an orange-and-yellow expeditionary parka whose triangles a helicopter rescue pilot could spot from miles away, if he should become stranded on a snowfield or an ice face. But I trusted his integrity and flexibility, and teased him that in one's fifties or sixties we didn't need to seek an abyss. We already *had* an abyss; we were poised. I knew a man who had climbed Kilimanjaro and never bothered to learn what tribe his bearers were from.

As for the Russians, they seemed to be groping for a national persona from which they could derive some decent pride, while winning a livelihood by transporting Americans—a people so supremely confident that they must seek artificial challenges—in civilized comfort into the utmost wilds. The captain was a subtle man, a thinker on such matters, and the second and third mates, Alexandr Savchenko and Evgeniy Levakov, in nice American sweaters, with European facial features, looked like they were from Minneapolis. Evgeniy said he'd seen duty as a paratrooper in Kazakhstan during his military tour and was a father, routing his pay of ten dollars or so per day directly home. Limbo, out here on the gelid deep, was better, he said, than the spiral of disorientation, corruption, and demoralization in Russia.

The first mate, named Slava Trukhanov, was a different sort, squat and bulky, a phlegmatically forceful Siberian with a lowish brow, a sloppy sweatshirt, and the look of one of Genghis Khan's troop commanders. He was a competent seaman, had served on a minesweeper, and had quickly picked up tourist English in this new posting, but he had little curiosity to use it, preferring to gaze flatly at the quiltwork of the sea or at his panels of instruments. Because of my love for Alaska and my nine visits there, I've sometimes flattered myself that, had I been a Muscovite writer exiled to Siberia, I might have survived better than some of the Russian intellectuals did. So I took our Slava to be the mayor of the Siberian village whose boundaries I was restricted to for purposes of this fantasy. And by watching him, I found him not too bad: certainly not a bad mate to the sailors, and we had one American he took a liking to. This was an Arizonan who ran rafts professionally down American, Siberian, and African rivers, a kind, burly man, thirtyish, now beginning to worry about what kind of conventional career he might switch to. (He told me that, true to my notion of "adventure companies" just being retreads of the old White Hunter days, they were now shooting crocodiles in the Zambezi River so that they could advertise raft trips that would be trouble-free). Slava took him down to watch Russian movies in the mess room and would impulsively walk over to him like an older brother to rub his wiry mop of hair and ask when he was going to get married and start a family like a good guy.

Across from Joinville Island is Petrel Cove on Dundee Island, which is strewn with leaky fuel barrels, rusty machinery, and collapsing tin and plywood shacks from the recent Chilean-Argentinean rivalry, and has a mile-long abandoned Argentinean naval airstrip on the stony beach, where we stretched our legs, in the absence of the fur and elephant and crabeater seals and nesting birds that must have made good use of it until not long ago. I missed the heavy, yeasty, barnyard smell of penguin dung on Joinville Island, however; the effervescent gabble.

En route to Paulet Island, just east of Joinville, we saw white icebergs that turned shark-blue underneath, like a double message, and flat little snow-covered floes that were peppered with resting black penguins, perhaps in the company of an eight-foot leopard seal, pale as a spotted ghost and sleeping off its last meal of another penguin that it had caught in a long, desperate chase underwater. Or the penguins' fellow passengers might be several silvery, greenish-gray crabeater seals, small-mouthed, sociable, and mild mannered. We also saw a sea-gray mamma Weddell's seal, a fish- and squid-eater midway between the leopard seal and the crabeater seals in size—a largish beast, lolling on a cake of ice, who Greg Myer speculated had probably weaned her single pup on an isolated beach only a couple of weeks before and now might be molting. She rolled over further on her itchy back in response to the apparition of our ship, in order to eye us better.

Paulet is a rookery for about six hundred thousand Adélie penguins, named for the wife of French explorer Admiral Jules Sebastian César Dumet d'Urville. Spiry yet already almost snowless, Paulet boasted a broad beach of slippery rocks and was marvelously raucous and smelly, seething with thousands of marching birds, or hollering paired-off sentinels, and trickly with melting runoff stained by red and green guano. The waves soughed mildly by comparison with the noise of this metropolis, once you got fifty yards up from the strand. Also, there were the remains of an emergency stone hut constructed in one quick week in March 1903 by twenty men led by the Norwegian whaler-explorer Carl Anton Larsen, more than sixty years after d'Urville's two voyages, when Larsen's ship had been caught and crushed in the ice. They'd roofed it with canvas, chinked it with guano, insulated it with sealskins, and killed and stacked eleven hundred Adélies to last them as food until spring. (Only one man didn't survive.)

Though a few raffish, piratical skuas swooped overhead, this was a place of yeasty prosperity—the penguins bravely stinky, bravely braying; and elegant, svelte blue-eyed shags (a kind of cormorant) nested in shoals among them. It's undoubtedly sentimental to ascribe "raffish" or "brave" behavior to birds, but sentiment in such a stark spot is endangered too. Those vanished whales by their absence had helped to feed this penguin city, and because the three common species of the Antarctic Peninsula have staggered nesting schedules—Adélies, chinstraps, and gentoos, in that order but often on different islands, two or three weeks apart—and dive to somewhat different depths as they search for fish and krill (gentoos as much as five hundred feet down), they dovetail more than they compete for food. The sumptuous, keening, terrifying funnel of life and death is layered like an underwater skyscraper for them. With ballasted wings, they peel off in sharply tangented Immelmann turns and barrel rolls, sideslipping, fishtailing, volplaning, whereas out under the canopy of the sky they have to either rest or nest.

Penguins surrendered their ability to fly in order to "fly" through the water better, propelled by their stubby wings, ruddering with their feet—rather in the same way that snakes gave up the capacity to walk in favor of crawling. In a hot antique jungle climate about one hundred and fifty million years ago, the lizards that eventually reinvented themselves as snakes found legs a hindrance in wriggling through the tangles, much as penguins, forty million years ago, experienced an icy climate change that capped the protein that they needed underwater. But whereas the vanishing jungle has left snakes in the unfortunate position of having made a Faustian bargain whose chits are falling due, the maritime penguin, in this particularly solipsistic weather system, is doing fine. Furthermore, the blubbery, bowling pin–shaped body and finlike wings it grew—the wings held stiffly out like arms for balance—and its big eyes and portly waddle, together with its black-and-white evening-dress costume, have won it potent friends, who may come in awfully handy if a penguin population crisis occurs over the harvesting of krill for human consumption someday. It's kind of unfair because snakes' leglessness is an esthetic curse, a death knell signaled in the Bible: *On your belly you will crawl.* But I like snakes and find that handling them soothes me like handling a string of worry beads or fingering a rosary might do. Their ancientness gives me pause, which is what nature does for us anyhow. And penguins, diving two hundred feet down or zestfully porpoising along the sea's surface at a speed that neatly matches the rhythm of their breathing, are offshoots of lizards too.

Our odd, alien party of penniless Murmansk seamen and moneyed Americans paying through the nose for two weeks of adventure steamed gently south through the night to Seymour Island, where the Argentineans have a big base of one hundred and fifty people supplied by air. From a discreet distance Seymour is a lengthy ridge of mudstone, sandstone, and limestone, which in midsummer looks to be the color of a lion's skin and is known for its remarkable petrified wood, and its fossils of an extinct marsupial, a five-foot penguin, and a marine dinosaur. The wind was up; we couldn't land, which disappointed our staff geologist, Wayne, who also leads tours of the Grand Canyon and up the Amazon with his friend Suzana. I hardly minded because we saw so many bachelor or bachelorette penguins swimming around, and occasional gray-green seals, and a minke whale afloat on the Weddell Sea, which we had now entered, plus the many stately bergs and darting birds. (Petrels derive their name from "Peter's birds," because in skimming they seem to walk on the water, like Saint Peter in the Gospel of Matthew.) Islands may appear more impressive when you lie just off them, imagining them, than if you actually land, with all the motley regimentation and boating rigmarole of going ashore.

"A piece of cake," the captain kept saying as we passed Snow Hill Island, which is larger but uninhabited by Argentineans or anyone else (though a Swedish geologist did spend two winters there ninety years ago). The Weddell Sea is named for James Weddell, the British sealer who penetrated it in 1823, and has a weighty feel. I'd supposed earlier that one might go to polar regions to recapitulate what, for example, Giovanni da Verrazano and Henry Hudson laid eyes on. But the sparse porpoising penguins vaulting like Frisbees out of the water and a few seals as noodgy as manatees couldn't lend Antarctica the plenitude of the Hudson River, circa 1524 or 1609. Instead we were in the midst of a Royal Navy of icebergs—pods and prides of them, next to which a whale looked mouse-sized—aircraft carriers one hundred feet high and therefore extending six hundred feet below the waterline, if you figured the physics of it. The biggest berg that has ever been sighted measured two hundred and eight miles by sixty miles, across its top. The Antarctic ice sheet itself contains 90 percent of the world's ice and is one and a half times the size of the United States, but nothing in nature looks more alien. One can't rightly compare icebergs to "castles," ice sculptures, vanilla frosting, or Soviet architecture, although, being human, we try to. Hard as concrete yet steadily melting, not water-colored or able to reflect the spectrum of sky colors that water does, not immutable like a cliff face, or green-clad and stream-chiseled like a mountainside, they're paradoxical. They lack what we think of as personality and in our mind's eye can throw a line to. Stately but disintegrating, cerulean perhaps in little streaks but as broad as a city block and impenetrably white, they represent the *Titanic* and death.

The waves whispered crisply against these numerous edifices. Close up, we'd see ancient grainy brownish veins in the ice, pitting it like smallpox and embodying snow crystals that may have fallen before Weddell or d'Urville or Larsen or Nathaniel Palmer—the sealer from Stonington, Connecticut, whom Americans credit with discovering the continent in 1820—had yet arrived. Thus it may be ice that's like the starlight which reaches us long after being launched, huge telegrams from prehistory yet geometrically squared off like goofy architecture, floating on the blue-black sea in gigantic blocks that are mostly an eerie, sanitary white. Originating from the Larsen, Ronne, and Filchner Ice Shelves, the bergs were positively everywhere, leaving less and less maneuvering room; and twenty-five miles short of the fog bank that marked the wall of pack ice, we turned back—though they continued to parallel us massively, like antiseptic, scar-faced monuments, till past nightfall, with periodic trios of tiny penguins as black as gnats the only speck of life, and a low pearly sky.

The map of Antarctica is tagged clear around with an extravagant foliage of names. Every cape or inlet, plateau or nunatak memorializes some ship's master, naturalist, whaler, sealer, naval officer, or adventurer lucky enough to have first clapped his weather eye upon it. Patrons, sweethearts, and home counties are also remembered, on glaciers, promontories, and islets, like a cacophony of testosterone— names hanging off the outline of the continent as thick as tassels, of people who had wanted to outlive death by flirting with it. There must have been other explorers who wished to leave only their footprints, but naturally we just know the hollerers. And so the map you study back home is very different from reality, where you hear no egos, only glaciers cracking, roaring, calving, splashing—or rumbling, thudding avalanches—and the cryptic hiss of the waves on the gravel.

I made the point to Gennadiy, and he repeated a quote from Genghis Khan: "The warrior who nails the sable skin on the wall after a battle is not the warrior who won the battle." I kept kidding him and Slava, Evgeniy, and Alexandr because the *Professor Molchanov*, its superstructure strung with electronic gizmos like a Christmas tree with baubles, *must* be a spy ship; and Gennadiy had hung off Cape Canaveral only a decade before, recording space-shot telemetry, then putting into Havana or Guinea-Bissau. Surely, too, our charts were so precise about depths because the Soviets had been hiding nuclear subs in these exotic waters?

"In the Arctic, yes," said Alexandr. "Not here. Too far."

"Then hunting subs," I insisted.

"Let me show you how you hunt subs," Alexandr said. He pulled out another chart, showing Siberia's Sea of Okhotsk, where lots of naval stuff was. His finger became an American submarine trying to sneak close, while his other hand was a Russian submarine cruising silently in a defensive position with big ears. "Subs hunt subs."

From the Weddell Sea we went through Erebus and Terror Gulf (named for the British warships James Ross employed on his terrific voyage of exploration in 1839–43) and through Antarctic Sound to the west side of the Peninsula, while I dreamt in swift jittery succession of crossing the Atlantic on a flimsy barge, and then of an imaginary lover who all of a sudden turned sadistic to me, and then of being captured crazily by Yahgan Indians in the Beagle Channel, until insomnia got me up to see the dawn.

We landed on Astrolabe Island, a toothy dot named for d'Urville's ship (and a former instrument of navigation), whose short beaches under modest, cuspy heights are a chinstrap penguin rookery. Tuxedoed, with the addition of a black line like a soldier's chinstrap, they were slightly more assertive than the Adélies, higher-headed, more attentive to us, and less dithery when we approached, waving their stubby, theatrical wings and gabbling in protest. They also were doing their "communal ecstatic display," as science calls it, which is neither communal nor entirely ecstatic, being in part a threat posture, but which also helps bind each penguin to its mate because the pitch of each bird's voice is unique. Chinstraps, too, are pebble lovers, and pebble stealers to improve their nests, and imprinted with the drive to return to the same beach every spring.

But they are thought to be more monogamous than the Adélies, which are adapted for the even tougher climates south of here, and therefore must be prepared to lose last year's mate.

Like Joinville Island, Astrolabe had the feel of a secret place, but was so small we saw no skuas. (According to David Campbell's excellent book on Antarctica, *The Crystal Desert*, a pair of skuas will patrol about ten thousand nesting penguins.) Eight Weddell seals, however, were resting in a row on a cushiony bed of snow while they shed their winter coats. Lying prone, they scarcely raised up to look at us, though they did groan a bit. There were also three shouldery fur seals established on separate flat patches of rock, apart from them—bachelor bulls who emphatically objected to our presence for territorial reasons by rearing up on their flexible flippers to offer us a maximum profile of strength. Unlike Weddell or crabeater or elephant seals, fur seals have land-worthy flippers and hind legs that fold forward under them and thus can propel them in an aggressive charge faster than a running man. Like sea lions, they have external ears and doglike heads, and bulk and height constitute a territorial display for them, even encompassing the rubbernecking posture of tall, two-legged tourists like us. They could be formidable on land, but since defending a special patch of rocks in beachmaster fashion is their purpose, they don't charge far. Indeed, some of the smartest sealers used bull fur seals as wardens of a kind, to pen the females on the beach, not letting them escape into the sea, while the sealers methodically killed and skinned them (a sealer might blind the bulls on their seaward side), until just the bulls were left, presiding over a harem of hideless carcasses, whereupon they themselves would be killed.

Terns and petrels also nest precariously on Astrolabe. The snow on the tide-washed beach was algae stained, and a blue berg was marooned in a tiny cove, among black seal-sized rocks that greatly outnumbered the seals.

Cruising across Bransfield Strait from Astrolabe to Deception Island, we admired the lovely dappled brown-and-white petrels skimming for krill, and the somnolent fur seals "jugging," as it's called—sleeping on their backs in the calm waves with their flippers folded over their chests, round as jugs, like sea otters in the north Pacific do. Indeed, Antarctic fur seal skins used to be shipped to China, where their coarse guard hairs were painstakingly plucked out so they could be passed off as much more valuable sea otter skins.

At intervals we encountered five separate pods of humpback whales, blowing in a leisurely fashion, then lifting their backs in loose unison, and their broad flukes with a seamlessly synchronized rolling motion, to dive. Side by side they did this, arching underwater and serenely reappearing at an unexpected angle, to exhale their misty sighs again. The mothers had calved off the coast of Colombia, Greg said, and swum down to gorge on the dense acres of krill nourished by the round-the-clock summertime daylight here. The babies' breathing (big creatures now) was impetuous, nervous, uneven, but the mothers' slow worldly sighs, forceful and vaguely wise, got to me, straight to the heart.

I live in a place—New England—where the volume and diversity of bird calls declines a bit more every spring. Fewer birds, fewer species, a weaker chorus—altogether, I would suspect, a third sparser than twenty-five years ago, which, in real time, is the blink of an eye. And that's part of why people shell out good sawbucks and frogskins to fly to

Thailand, Tanzania, the Amazon, or Antarctica to see what's left. At home, for wildness, I hike into terrain so high that no real-estate developer has been interested yet, so the idea that the whole White Continent is still not owned seems quite incredible. But twenty-six nations have set up "scientific" stations here to fly their flags and pre-position themselves for a land grab if policies change.

Frogskins and sawbucks were terms for money in my younger days, when people sometimes ate bullfrogs and still sawed firewood: there were so many trees and frogs around. Greenbacks reminded them of a frog's skin, and the X on a ten-dollar bill of a sawhorse's legs. People might have a dried rabbit's foot attached to their key ring for good luck, and liked it when a good rat snake took up residence under the house, or if there were bats in the belfry of the church up the street to keep the summer's crop of flying bugs in control. Nature was a natural condition—not a churchless religion for its devotees, twinned with jogging, meditation, Walkmans, Prozac, or whatnot, but best accessible to those with plush incomes. We on the *Professor Molchanov* were members of the green groups, the Audubon Society, Nature Conservancy, Greenpeace, Sierra Club, Wilderness Society, World Wildlife Fund—though my early years of struggle as a writer were bankrolled by a small inheritance from my mother's mother, whose money came from logging operations among the primeval Douglas firs of Grays Harbor in Washington. What would now seem to be museum-piece trees thus founded my beginnings. And with our stomachs full of flounder, sole, shrimp, our oil-based synthetic clothes, oxblood shoes, Honda gas tanks, freeways, swimming pools and ranch houses, all wrung from the earth—the million miles of swamp and forest drained, stripped, or paved over—we *still* wear billions of frogskins on our backs and pay for our accoutrements in sawhorses.

We travelers were all pondering not this, but the quandaries of grief or a job change, how it felt to get old and retire, our marriages or sexual chevaux-de-frise, our guilt and pain. The power-company president from Iowa and I were thinking of our newly dead wives, and a friend of mine was dying of Lou Gehrig's disease, and four or five others had died of hemorrhaging or carcinogenic catastrophes before having had their proper say in the world: with more books to write, more friendship to give, and kids who still needed a great deal more of their time. Life is so very precious while you have it, yet comes with a kind of biblical itch, a scabies patch on the back that never quite quits, but keeps you going. Antarctica is mostly entropic, on the other hand, lifeless, the edge of the void, where the sweet rain that elsewhere wets our lips and keeps us alive is cruelly crystalline, yet a feast for the eyes. That we could so profoundly enjoy the lifeless sight of ice is part of the mysterious double dimension that makes us puzzlingly human. Life had chafed us—whether with polio or widowerhood or sexual abuse (as one person hinted) or sieges of stuttering and semiblindness, in my case—and it was a tonic to stray so far.

Deception Island is a volcano's caldera, an aficionado's ultimate destination, if you start from Cape Horn in a steel-hulled ketch and get across six hundred miles of the world's roughest water, then zero in on the correct beachless dot of cinder-colored rock, tall and forbidding, till you sail round it and—presto!—spy an opening in the walls like a hidden slot that is ten fathoms deep and wide enough for even a cruise ship to slide inside. A splendid anchorage, a lake of seawater five miles long and three miles wide, awaits you there, with reddish-brown ashy beaches—and chinstraps nesting on them—rising all the way to the crater's rim, where a few pocket glaciers strewn with recently exploded ash linger year-round, set off by yellowish patches of lichen. At the far end of this peaceful oval is a handsome bowl where the water is hundreds of fathoms deep, but emerging from a slit in the lip of the shore is a little hot spring where tourists take a dip that qualifies them to say when they get home that they swam in the waters of Antarctica.

Nathaniel Palmer, the Connecticut sealer twenty-one years old who went on to run guns to Simón Bolívar in what is now the nation of Colombia, and later helped to invent the clipper ship and grew wealthy trading with China, discovered Deception Island in November 1820. It became a safe harbor for other sealers and soon a major whaling station, the rusting detritus of which remains in Whalers' Bay—barracks, ash heaps, hangars, huts, hulks of machinery. But the austere symmetry of the crater is mesmerizing, a sanctuary where you might freeze and starve, but take a while to realize it. Walking about, we met a couple of Spanish military men and some Argentinean sailors and scientists and the daring crew of a sailboat that had lost its mainsail under way from Buenos Aires. British and Chilean scientists sometimes camp here, too. During the last eruption a quarter of a century ago, they'd fled with burning shirts, rescuing one another.

We cruised through the night to the Antarctic mainland, south of Trinity Island, to a thirteen-person Argentinean research station called Primavera, perched like a couple of close, colorful dots in a hook-shaped bay of purple water surmounted by shelving glaciers and other perpendicularities that looked a bedazzling white. It was stirringly sumptuous, steeply mountainous, in a smothering surplice of maybe a dozen or twenty different shades of ice or snow—crystal and diamond and custardy egg-white—in long schlossing drifts and billowy dunes, illuminated by bright effervescent sunshine. The visible peaks hinted that others must lie back beyond, while the rustling, inky water at our prow bobbed with dozens of floes that had just cracked off the sheer walls. Though lush in the way that green can be lush, it was also eye-popping because it was so white. On deck, a sort of prolonged quiet ecstasy possessed Gloomy Guses like Chuck and me, who had passed the half-century mark with many prior adventures and perhaps too many memories to process new stuff properly. We were smiling like babies.

White can indeed be luxuriant, a color for weddings and royalty and special people, of ermine and satin and lilies, but also of tusks and hypothermia, a celebrity color, or the ghastly pallor of death. These little glaciers with brown nunataks sticking out of them, calving blue and creamy bergs into the bay, had left one pitch of ground that thawed to bare scree every spring. The Argentinean scientists—two women were in charge—lived in red board buildings set on stilts above the permafrost, amidst a gentoo colony and two hundred pairs of nesting skuas that ranged out elsewhere, and sheathbills, which are another scavenger, and some Cape petrels and Wilson's storm petrels and Antarctic terns. Altogether since the camp's establishment in 1953, eleven species of birds, three types of seals, twenty-five mosses, forty varieties of algae, and a hundred lichen have been totted up here, plus two inconspicuous inch-high kinds of grasses and two sorts of insects: namely, feather lice and seal mites.

Three months is not an intolerable stretch to be stranded here, said the middle-aged cook, who volunteers every year, and the radioman and Buenos Aires scientist-intellectuals agreed, referring jokingly to a doctor posted at another base who had made himself mildly famous by setting fire to the place in order to be airlifted out before his enlistment was up. The cook offered us a hospitality gourd of maté, a herbal tea, and cookies to pass around, and Chuck gave them their mail from Ushuaia and a box of fresh vegetables. Our engine-room crew ferried some of them across the bay in a Zodiac to check experimental equipment that they had placed there but couldn't visit because their government hadn't provided them with a boat. We passengers went putt-putting in two other Zodiacs, scouting the bluish crisp floes dusted with sparkling corn snow. Half a dozen crabeater seals were snoozing on these, their green-tea or sea-turtle coats marred by two-foot scars that dated to when they were pups and a leopard seal had grabbed and tried to devour them. The two leopard seals we drifted upon were more alert, and one opened and chopped his big jaws at our approach, as a bear will do when circled. His camouflage was different, olive or charcoal-gray on top and pale ashy gray on the underside, with the eponymous spots. Twice the length of a man, he had a mouth three or four times as wide as a crabeater's, though his incisors were shorter than a bear's or a leopard's, and he had very large shoulders and flippers for purposes of pursuit. His face was grimly primitive looking, not so much like a mammal's as like a python's or an ancient sea reptile's.

Antarctica is a relic formed three or four hundred million years ago when the upper Paleozoic supercontinent Gondwanaland began breaking up into Africa, the subcontinent of India, South America, and then Australia, as Antarctica drifted south. The climate had been so temperate that marsupials may have walked to Australia from their North American origins by means of the land mass that now constitutes Antarctica. But the land bridges vanished eighty-five million years ago, and four million years ago the present ice sheets started to coalesce. Afterward there could be no grasslands or forests for castaways to colonize, no Eskimos or Indians to glower now at tour ships coming to this appendage of the Andes.

From Primavera we sailed south through Gerlache Strait to Charlotte Bay, opposite Brabant Island. Our stalwart helmsman, Vasiliy, sported a T-shirt with BOSS stenciled on it, and the supple-faced boatswain, Vladimir, and the comely, skinny seaman who had been nicknamed "Mr. Blue-eyes" by some of our livelier passengers both wore other American giveaways. The sea had its disciplines and manifold moods that thankfully overrode the daily shortwave squawk of Moscow news. Glistering and platinum white or navy blue, it heaved and slammed, causing our ornithologist, Greg, to miss his newborn son and reflect caustically on "breeding males and nonbreeding males" vis-à-vis penguins and people (he himself had been gladly changing since his marriage); and our Boston bank loan officer to plan a trip to Slovenia, where she had ancestors, and Chuck to speak of his mentor, the English teacher killed on Mount Everest ("a little death on a big mountain") and his return here next month with a boatload of macho glacier climbers. On this trip we figured more than half of us had snapped more than a thousand photos apiece. It was like a disease, the bending, limping, stooping, gesticulating, view-finding, lens-twiddling Saint Vitus' dance that people engaged in, as though their cameras were their children and the effort was to give them an emotional experience. Lens settings, like frequent-flier mileage—some said they even bought their groceries by credit card to pile up extra mileage, one for every dollar billed if you had the right card, and then if you got divorced they'd let you split your miles—was a topic of irrepressible appeal, after the attentive pieties of the panorama had been disposed of: like coming home.

In our exhilaration at these quick takes, these brushes with exotica for which we'd come so far, we felt closer to one another as well, though so random a collection of people—the go-go San Diego couple with impeccable tans; the gentle Iowan who had risen on the ladder at his power company not as an engineer but in personnel; the Clorox chemist whose wife kept apologizing affectionately because she didn't "like chemicals"; the bearded, boyish, muscular river runner from the Arizona desert; the polio sufferer who had become a sex therapist; and Chuck, in a cowpuncher's hat, charging about like a bison. The Argentineans had posted a road sign at Primavera saying they were still 2,870 kilometers from the South Pole, and only 1,109 from Ushuaia, but I was reading Apsley Cherry-Garrard's *Worst Journey in the World*, probably the best of the Antarctica journals, about a ski trip across the winter ice in 1911 in search of emperor penguin eggs. (Emperors lay their eggs in the winter.) Also Ernest Shackleton's and Robert Falcon Scott's books about their heroic treks. Scott may possibly be said to have died because he didn't appreciate dogs. That is, he tried using Siberian ponies and motor sledges to pull his loads and they broke down, whereas his rival in the race to the Pole, Roald Amundsen, relied on fifty-two sled dogs.

And I'd brought along the diary of a distant cousin I'd recently gotten my hands on. He was an aspiring foreign correspondent who was murdered at twenty-nine in Inner Mongolia in 1905, and his voice on the page sounds a bit like mine. He'd left college to enlist in the Spanish-American War in 1898. Afterward, he moved from serving in Cuba to the Philippines to work as an administrator in the mountains of Luzon with Igorot tribesmen. But then reports of the Russo-Japanese War in 1904 juiced him up, and off he set via Ceylon, where he picked up a French adventurer as a traveling companion, a bogus or cashiered army lieutenant.

My cousin John was handicapped and doubtless partly driven by fluctuating but daily attacks of asthma, much as I'd been as a young writer-traveler by a bad stutter, except when his exuberant absorption in his surroundings distracted him from fretting about it, and therefore it let up on him. And as with me later, life may have seemed such an emergency anyway, such a leap of faith even while staying at home, that he was prepared to trust all manner of people when launching himself on a trip. The Frenchman unfortunately was a mistake. After they'd left Ceylon for China— and then headed up to Peking to cross Inner Mongolia and Manchuria on horseback to reach the battle areas by land— John's diary gradually becomes uneasy, jittery, scared, though his tone also sounds throttled by the knowledge that his companion may be reading it. His money and passport have been stolen. He suspects, first, some villagers, but later his wording is elliptical and panicky, and the journal breaks off. His body was never discovered, but his baggage was left in the last hamlet they'd stopped in. The Frenchman thereupon disappeared, after cashing John's letters of credit by forging his signature, back in Ceylon.

We marveled at the blowing, fluking whales in trios, pairs, quartets, blue-black, bundled in the gray water. The youngest animals stood practically on their tails, "spy-hopping" as it's called, to get a gander at us, the mother maybe prompting them for educational purposes. Then, since they can't climb out on the ice floes like a seal, they'd nap in the water till our thrum woke them again. The Weddell seals, fish eaters that stay here all winter—chewing breathing holes in the ice instead of migrating to open water as the other mammals do—are little fellows next to the whales, but have more heft and rather a lovely sea-and-ice coloring and a rounder, comelier mouth than the moss-yellow, krill-grubbing crabeaters, which are thought to outnumber them by about twenty-five to one.

Growlers and discolored bergy bits slid by, and one splendiferous berg, big as a stadium, though quite stately, with bitty penguins tossing themselves about its ledgey flanks. Two minke whales escorted our bow, and all around, once we had reached the larger perspective of Charlotte Bay, we confronted a gargantuan semicircle of glacier mountains, bulging buxom and highly tiered, with numerous fresh bergs that had just chunked off and now clustered about us, church-sized, gymnasium-sized, and thus far so innocent of the ocean that they were sharp-edged, sugar-white, vanilla-new. Charlotte Bay is one of the most beautiful sights on earth, equivalent to Mount McKinley or Lake Como, though crunchy with provisionality because you could so easily die here and the very profile of the ice is changing continually. White as virginity, white as a funeral, yet so crisp I nearly wanted to embrace the icescape and be set on shore to take my chances and entrust the snowfield with my infinitesimal life. Individually we fugued, whether with binoculars or cameras, in the midst of this summer scene so starched, succinct, and crystalline, although punctuated by cannon booms from the glaciers' snouts and bursts of katabatic wind. Wellman Glacier, Bayly Glacier, Mount Johnston, and the Foster Plateau going up seven thousand feet, stood close. Despite the cold breeze on deck, I grinned until my mouth ached.

We sailed on and stopped at a place called Portal Point to look at a peak-roofed, two-room abandoned hut provisioned with 1950s tabloids and tinned foods for the British exploring teams that had holed up here. Built of wood and tar paper, with bunks, shelves, cozy glass windows, and cement blocks outside to anchor it against the wind, it seemed homey in this summer interlude. Three crabeater seals lay on their backs in the side yard wriggling to rub off their molting fur. Some gentoos were also about, placid, convivial birds with pretty white eyebrows, salmon legs, and orange bills. That they are unafraid of us is of course part of their quaint appeal, in a larger world where all other wild creatures flee. The water temperature at Ushuaia had been twelve degrees centigrade, and had fallen to three degrees as we reached the islands off Antarctica, but the pods of orca whales that will pop penguins into their mouths in about the same way we eat shrimp, and the fleets of bergy bits upon which the birds can float and hide, and the surge of storms under the theater of the sky were not digitalized. (Even for reptiles there is immense leeway, if they know their habitat intimately, not just in how much they manage to eat and how long they survive their preda-

tors, but how well they take advantage of or cushion themselves against temperature change.)

From Charlotte we sailed to Cuverville Island, another
glacier and fjord spectacle, where we anchored and napped
through the wee hours. Four Britishers were tenting on the
beach between two penguin rookeries. By occupation they
were a moss botanist, a penguin ornithologist, a geographer,
and a lawyer-administrator. The geographer's task was to
map people-movements as precisely as possible, because
two thousand tourists a year debarked from cruise ships
here and one rookery was kept off-limits to them as a "control" area, while the other was left open for freelance mean-
dering. Then at the end of the season the penguin and moss
biologists would total up the damage that had been done.
Though I approved of the idea, I immediately skewed their
statistics a trifle by reboarding our ship when I found out
that I was being mapped, it was such a comedown from the
era of Shackleton, Amundsen, and Scott.

Ronge Island, across a gap, was not being mapped. A fur
seal bull acted as beachmaster, swelling up and posturing to
nearly a man's height on a rock that he'd picked, while two
cows dozed on the gravel nearby. Both gentoos and chinstraps were nesting higher up, their colonies contributing a
farty assertion of life's pungency to the added scent of seal
urine and the seaweed's piquant smell. Penguin tracks ran
uphill through the snow to where their chicks were waiting
to be fed, though the doughty parents had to concentrate
their ungainly steps into trenchlike paths between outcrops
of rock that would have been impassable otherwise. And it
was on these "highways" that tourists could cause the
deaths of penguins unintentionally by punching cylinders in
the snow with their boots, into which the descending chicks

would fall and never be able to scramble out, and within which the adults too—waddlers almost as helpless as chicks ashore—might get trapped.

Out in the channel, a mamma humpback whale breached, blowing like a hippo, a robust personable sound, as confident as a matriarchal elephant, only more so. She was about fifty feet long, rather skinny, with the big calf that had been draining her now swimming, spouting and throwing its flukes into the air, then leaving its swirling "footprints" on the surface of the water alongside. Her breath exploded like a cow elephant's, communicating her peremptory pleasure in the ease of this glorious midsummer's day. We weren't harassing them yet in the Zodiacs, so there didn't seem to be a complaining or protesting tone to it, just a jumbo emphasis upon how independent, vigorous, and good she felt—a booming exhalation nearly on a par with the distant avalanches and the glaciers that we heard noisily splitting.

When we did start following the two, their movements, though not frightened, became constrained. The blowing lost its sense of jubilation. Luckily, before we'd chased them far, two leopard seals began to investigate us, which afforded our twenty photographers a worthy distraction. These "polar bears of the South," eight-hundred-pounders, ten feet long, trailed and examined us, rolling closely under the boats, then rising slowly out of the water at arm's length, head to head, even more predatory than we were. With their leopard-spotted chests and grimly primitive heads, as huge-mouthed and simple in configuration as the python I keep at home (only, a hundred times heavier than he is), they re-examined and inspected us further. Under the boats and up, again under and up, and swiveling to face us in a lithe, leisurely, whimsically unbrotherly fashion, these penguin seizers that slap and shake a bird clear out of its skin before swallowing it gave us a thorough once-over before going their merry way. We were uncommonly silent.

We left the whales and seals to visit another abandoned British survey-team hut and, after passing a German research vessel, the *Polar Star*, steamed for three hours down Gerlache Strait and Neumayer Channel to Port Lockroy, a former whaling station in a sheltered inlet on Wiencke Island, where several 1940s structures remain. Also, somebody had assembled a composite humpback whale skeleton from scattered vertebrae and other bones. We posed for a group photo in front of this. Thousands of dowdy, pretty gentoos were nesting vociferously in the vicinity, and a few blue-eyed shags—pointy-beaked, fast-flying, and infinitely trimmer birds with eyes like tiny bull's-eye targets—were feeding fish to their young in the hyperalert manner of other cormorants, although hugging the fringe of the fussy gentoos' site for the relative safety this offered their own nests against the skuas' attacks.

On Jougla Point the penguins wobbling down to the sea to obtain a meal for their hollering chicks were squeezed into a narrow aisle between the rocks that we were sitting on and the rocks that were their nesting ground. I felt sorry for them, especially when some of our photographers spilled into their three-foot passageway for close-ups and a hungry leopard seal appeared at the beach end, looping and somersaulting in the water, barely bothering to conceal his presence as he waited impatiently for the poor penguins to run our gauntlet and reach him. The jostling in the colony above us, too, was threatening to knock a couple of chicks off their nests and into oblivion. Every twenty minutes or so an avalanche on the mainland would roar, and the gusts of wind kicked up quite cold, as if to remind us where we really were. Fog was moving in, with a nice "fogbow"—a yellow arc like a rainbow—just parting enough to remind us that black cliffs lay all around.

The tension broke when one of our number, a computer guy who had touched me from the start in his dorky isolation, which sometimes reminded me of myself, got sprayed with penguin feces by a nervous mother, and suddenly became everybody else's pent-up butt. People who had never expressed the slightest ridicule of him now howled at his plight and thus made him yet more frantic to wash it off. So he got his clothing wet in the icy ocean while trying to. It was purgative. We cleared out of the penguins' navigating space, and everyone got washed clean of their own geekiness for the time being.

Suppering as we passed the end of Anvers Island, Chuck said he and Lynn keep a van all stocked with sleeping bags, a stove, and food so that they can take right off from the office in California for camping trips. He said it was no good believing that opposites attract; he'd tried that in a previous marriage. Lynn added, however, that soon after they had started dating he'd gone off for a month and a half, guiding a climb of Aconcagua, and lost so much weight that when he came back, he had a different body to get used to. With a barometer strapped to his wrist, and orange and yellow triangles dramatically marking his parka for rescue aircraft to home in on—lurchy, abrupt, electric, compulsive—he seemed to want to launch projects beyond our paltry capacities. Oldish folk, desk jockeys, we irritated *me* too.

On past Doumer Island, we reached Lemaire Channel, between Booth Island and the mainland, at sixty-five degrees, six minutes (the Antarctic Circle, again, is sixty-six and one-half degrees). This was farther south than we had gotten in the Weddell Sea, and it was gorgelike enough to take your breath away. Toothy nunataks stuck up out of the cascading ice on Booth Island, which rose more than sixty-five hundred feet above the water on our starboard side, while just to port the mainland mountains went higher, above vertiginous chutes and endless carpets of snow.

I was at the bow a lot, no longer afraid of jumping over. I was too happy, and besides, such incongruous, gratuitous self-absorption would have struck me as absurd. People do kill themselves in beautiful settings, like the Golden Gate Bridge, but they probably have more compelling reasons and the place itself becomes a kind of still life or stage setting for gruesome self-dramatization. This was not San Francisco Bay, arty and softly lit for amateur theatricals. This was a primeval grindstone, as grand as Genesis, or Genesis in reverse.

Death loses part of its sting, and therefore interest, when I am outdoors. But my wife, raised in the city, had been quite frightened in the out-of-doors. She was an indoor person—it was of course part of our problem. Even on her brief visits to our country place, she seldom stepped outside. Talk was her life's blood, scintillating and warm of heart, so that our lack of a phone there, which was a plus to me, was a hardship from her standpoint. And indeed when I think of other friends I miss and mourn, it wasn't nature they drew their faith from, it was great music and classic literature, or an Irish effusion of friendship. It was the pleasure of lazing and lovemaking, schmoozing and eating, a webwork of arcane loyalties. Curiosity and a bracing cynicism sustained some of them, or love of work, love of family, or the hope of love and sex and fame and money. I haven't seen the peace which passeth understanding prevail in many people after they've been told that they should prepare to die. Instead they naturally feel a tearful, gnawing frustration—their youngest child not yet out of college, their best books, perhaps, not yet written; and to both the precious child and in the projected book, *so much left unsaid!* My former wife, a writer, had been one of these.

Nature doesn't speak for you afterward, if you haven't had your say in the world. But nature, if you place your faith in it, dilutes that compulsion and other vanities. The wiggling gleam of flowing water, the romantic disk of the moon, the soothing enigma of starlight, the sight of wind-blown grass, whirling leaves, and large-crowned trees, the smell of woods soil, the extraordinary comfort, both emotional and physical, delivered by the sun, are free. We may have different enthusiasms. I like to look at animals without attempting to shoot them, for instance, and prefer to look up at mountains, not down from their summits. I love the densest cities—believing nature also encompasses human nature in Cairo, New York, or Bombay—whereas you may think great cities are an eczema. But these distinctions are as immaterial to nature as whether or not you carry a swagger stick. What matters is how long you're alive to what's going on.

Lemaire Channel was our destination, a fitting turnaround. The channel funneled narrower, plushly implacable, till you might think a little fishing boat would be a safer vehicle. Winding through such savage scenery, I was mesmerized. My eyes glissaded down extravagant piled-up choked snowdrifts, ivory ice, jagged ebony rock in giddy outcroppings, and a silence whose match I might never know again. A hardy band of us, mostly women, stood a long while at the bow despite the cold: the Boston banker with the wonderfully muscular arms and legs and a tough-love mouth who had compared our trip to a space voyage; my friend the sales clerk from Chicago, with a taste for swashbuckling men and desperate romance; the video packager with the haunting, thwarted-looking beauty; and the slight, grizzled Bayer engineer from Cologne who had been in sixty countries and taken fifteen thousand color slides. I knew this was an isolation I would never see equaled in my lifetime, not in the wildest inhabited place.

At a pocket in the channel between the cliffs of ice, the *Professor Molchanov* most carefully turned around, though our passage toward the Shangri-la of ultimate coldness could have continued if we had wished to take it. I'd thought daily of the professor, in handcuffs and leg shackles, painfully hungry, dying of a pistol shot from a countryman in the cruel snow within sight of his beloved St. Petersburg, and the contrasting fact that the danger I had feared in signing up for this jaunt to Antarctica was not of sinking or freezing or catching pneumonia or any other old-fashioned natural danger but the silly, self-hexing squirrel trap of suicide, which seemed to exemplify the diminishment of our self-indulgent age. Cascades of ice, the bottomless ocean, and two skeletons of rock to hang the ice from on each side were all we had, but the honeycomb of frigid fjords and inlets, the aeolian solitude, and our sense of traveling on the brink of borrowed time lent glory to the procession of recapitulated sights.

There was a saying in the nineteenth century, when people returned from a gold rush or a war or some arresting sortie along the edge of the frontier: *I have seen the Elephant.* It is, of course, a paler time. We have fewer "elephants," and try to synthesize a great many faux ones for each that really exists. Many of us have logged more mileage than Captain Cook in a mathematical sense, and childhood has no wondrous centerpiece, such as a glimpse of a one-ring-circus elephant by torchlight at the county seat must have been. Yet even so, and even on a package tour, the traveler does retain the final initiative in the privacy of his mind. You *can* see Antarctica and allow it to register. I'm not sure how much I succeeded at this. Like everything now, it's a matter of subtle ambiguity, of silence amid cacophony. But I stayed outside, both for the joy I felt and to give my mind a chance, until we had left Lemaire again.

ROADLESS REGIONS:
A JOURNAL SAMPLER

———◆———

M.'s father liked to eat food companionably off other people's plates when suppering with his friends or family, and might exchange shoes with a man whose feet were about his size—in token of friendship would go home wearing his.

Moose tracks tilt in deep snow according to which direction the animal was headed in. You can measure with an ax handle which way the tilt lies.

Emil Gilels: the piano's notes like marbles spilling, and then he gathers them in.

What we possibly need is a new variety of the neutron bomb, designed to kill people and leave behind not empty buildings but the rest of Creation.

"That's the chair you were nursed in," my mother tells me one day, disconcertingly. Speaking of an old flame of hers, she pumps her dress over her heart with two fingers to show how it had throbbed.

Story about a man's tie to his first wife, who lives not far from his neighborhood and hangs a towel in her window for him to see as he drives by if all is not going well.

Indians of certain tribes wrestled for the available wives before going out for the winter on their separate traplines. Strength superseded wealth in these contests, but the winner was sometimes the smaller man, if he had shaved his head and greased his ears so his opponent had nothing to grab onto.

A story told from the viewpoint of a Galápagos tortoise being carried upside down on the deck of a sailing ship to be eaten later on, and lined in a row with others, equally unable to turn over.

A story about a man who hires a baby-sitter for himself. He is exhausted, drained out, simply wants to be sat with (not prostitution).

The Greeks pursued by the Persian general Tissaphernes sacrificed a bull, a wolf, a bear, and a ram in order to escape.

A wit who after each clever comment he makes wears the triumphant but tiptoe expression of a percussionist after clashing the cymbals.

By boiling caribou horns for two days and then skimming off the white stuff that congeals on top and salting it to taste, you can make "butter" in the far taiga.

A lynx I saw in late spring crossing the road was shedding its winter fur, and so on its legs it appeared to be wearing galoshes.

I've noticed that the best dogs have a taste for vegetation, sampling it often, with much enjoyment, nibbling and chewing it, wagging their tails as if it were a tonic.

My apple trees are blossoming, a week after the chokecherries. Today I went up the east branch of the Nulhegan River to a roadless region. The trees creaked like a fox's bark. Saw coon tracks where there were frogs' jelly-and-eggs or tiny tadpoles in the puddles. Saw a merganser on the river, and a deer and a fisher, both nimbly quartering away from me. The fisher's back looped up into a high curve as it smelled my dog Bimbo's tracks. Saw a little bird picking the eyes out of a dead bird of the same species to recover its proteins.

Hiked today for five hours up the west branch of the Moose River to its head and watershed near what was once the Rhubarb Logging Camp, between East and Starr mountains. From there, one can go on over to Madison Brook and down that to Paul Stream and turn south along Granby Stream to Granby. Or from Madison Brook one can veer north to South America Pond and on to Notch Pond; then to the Nulhegan and up one of its branches; or, instead, climb West Mountain and go down to Bloomfield. These are all trips I hope to carry out. Saw lady slippers in the woods. Saw a porcupine sitting in a young poplar tree in an alder swamp, balancing itself with one hand while the other held a leaf to its mouth. Looked like a yellow-backed baboon.

Ephraim Webster, white prototype of Fenimore Cooper's Natty Bumppo, was a pioneer fur trader near what is Syracuse. Married two Indian girls, telling second he would stay married to her as long as she remained sober. But twenty years later a considerable white settlement had grown up and he wanted to marry into it and shed his old Indian squaw. Tried repeatedly to make her drunk, but she avoided his ruses. Finally succumbed to whiskey concealed in milk, and left next morning, and died brokenhearted.

Beware of a man who wears jockey shorts and uses shoe trees, M. was told, and agrees.

A cat's eyes are ten times as efficient as a man's at night, but a horned owl's are ten times more efficient than a cat's. Mice bound along awkwardly, too light for their legs, which makes them as jerky as butterflies and sometimes saves them.

> "I hope it is said when I am dead
> His sins were scarlet but his books were read."
>> (Hilaire Belloc)

An Indian family in New England needed an estimated six thousand temperate acres to support itself.

"A plump wife and a big barn
Does no man any harm."

"Mackerel sky,
Not long dry."

"Beware of that man, be he friend or brother,
Whose hair is one color and his beard another."

Pat R.'s mafioso uncle is so generous that he refuses to have his hospitality declined. Pushed the face of a visiting little boy into a bowl of spaghetti the little boy didn't want to eat. The uncle has never been caught for the big things he did, and "doesn't have to carry a gun," only the smaller things, except that he has had to serve seven years for personally beating up cops.

Rifka is built big in the hips with a low center of gravity, such that she bounces back from life's blows like one of those bowling-pin punching bags that can't be knocked down.

Went to the fights at the Garden with Vic Ziegel. Saw Walter Seeley outpoint a Korean who at twenty-seven has won seventy-four fights, lost twenty-five, and drawn thirteen. "He fought first with rattles," Vic says. Sat next to fighter who retired in 1952 after killing another middleweight (fought three more times to give the purses to the widow). Now is a sales manager for Rheingold. "Punch up!" he keeps yelling to Seeley, meaning a left hook to the belly, which happens to have been his own best punch ("like lifting a garage door," says Vic). But Seeley, as we later learn, broke his left hand in the second round. This man is also a movie adviser and his eyes and features were used as a model by Marlon Brando's makeup men for *On the Waterfront*. Tells stories of itinerant guy who fought Primo Carnera thirty times under nearly that many names around the country, and of "loan job" championships, held just for the interval between two fights. The Korean taps Seeley's back when they clinch, as the ref would do, but is waiting to sucker punch him if he thinks it's the ref. Paddy Flood comes over to greet Vic, and meets the one man he ever lost to in his own career, who is heaving chicken crates now at Hunts Point Market in the Bronx—but as the guy keeps saying, "I was too strong for you, right, Paddy? Just too strong." "A nutcase," Paddy mutters to us. Another Paddy, under indictment for attempted murder of his landlord with a hammer, strolls up to talk about the good old days in the ring with Bobo Olson or Paddy DeMarco, and the groupie girls at the training camps. Paid "nigger" sparring partners $10 a round and then tried to knock their blocks off. DeMarco was a "billy goat" because he butted. Our new Paddy got so angry he tried to hand him a box full of tin cans, as fitting for him to eat, and called him a "fucking guinea" (being Irish).

The Louvre is named for its site, which was originally a wolf breeding ground.

Dog trots along with a smile on his puss and his tongue dangling from the side of his mouth like a piece of red meat that he's grabbed.

Indian kids slid on sleds made from a buffalo's jaws tied to its rib cage.

I find in the woods at the edge of a field among broken car parts, in half of a broken wine bottle, a shrew's nest with many mouse skulls.

Story of a huge flock of ducks that settle on a cold lake, and the lake freezes over during the night, and in the morning the ducks fly away south carrying the whole lake with them.

December's is the Cold Moon, January's is the Wolf Moon, February's is the Hunger Moon. Squaw winter precedes Indian summer.

My sperm, when I was young and strong and masturbating, used to fly up and hit me in the chin. Maybe thirty million sperm cells manufactured a day.

W., the son of a Fifth Avenue dowager, a Yalie who helped my midwestern father successfully penetrate the thickets of New York social life as a young Wall Street lawyer, ended his life dying of gangrene on a Brooklyn side street due to having taken a leg injury to a chiropractor and otherwise not treated it, while buying gas station sites for a local distributor.

"You think when you're dying you'll at least have some original thoughts, but no, your thoughts just go round and round," Shoshana says.

Melville's pleasure at feeding pumpkins to his cow between stints at the "Whale book."

Two types of writers fall short: those who write well about unimportant things, and those who write badly about important things. Then there are the experimenters, who never get their bags unpacked, just try out techniques for when they'll begin.

At the dentist's, how like two monkeys we are: one with his mouth wide open, the other helpfully picking inside.

Archie the bartender moving his sister over in the bed they shared when they were little so it would seem *she* had wet the sheets. His father, to box with him, would put on one glove and smoke a cigar and say Knock it out of my mouth.

Women are drawn to a writer for his intensity but will leave him for the same reason, said James T. Farrell.

The very new rich have two first names; the very old rich two last names.

Two kinds of men: those who in adolescence were good with jalopies, and those who caught fish or turtles.

A nightmare: man stands in a corner vomiting, and when he is finished and turns around it is apparent that he has vomited his face off. It remains on the ground.

The human body uses about as much energy at rest as a 100-watt lightbulb.

Grave marker on the frontier: a saucepan upright.

Frank Crowther died of pills last night with his invariable plastic gloves on, hands folded on his chest, with notes left to be opened by his bar friends. His whole body was so inflamed with a skin ailment that (a bachelor in his late forties) he could no longer take his clothes off in front of a woman, he claimed. On the wall were pictures of him with Cary Grant, the Kennedys, and so on. Always liked to say he moved in many circles, high and low (ours being the low).

In the cold north of Europe, life was thought to have originated from the divine cow Audhumla's licking of frozen stones.

Saliva is alkali, stomach juice acid.

A hurricane may begin from the wingbeat of a single seagull, suggests Eric Kraus, a meteorologist.

Saw Robert Lowell in Central Park by the Mall looking very eager, alive, rhapsodic, his gangling body moving fast as he tried to see all of the bicycling kids at once—finally slouched on a bench to watch at his leisure. Six months before at same spot had looked muddled, sick, mumbly.

Teaching at Sarah Lawrence or any other women's college is more like being a eunuch than having a harem (as some people think) because no actual sex occurs. Rather, one is acclimating very young women for a future with other men, and you notice that although the female teachers remain as they were, the tenured male teachers become silken and lenient, soft and dreamy, "luxurious," limited.

Oct. 17, rabbit hounds around this notch all day long, and Paul Doyle's bear hounds too, till, about five o'clock, yet more yapping sounded from uphill. I was so riled by then I thought maybe *this* time I'll knock one of those hounding dogs over. But no, instead, it's thirty geese, up six hundred feet in a wavy checkmark, flying south.

Thoreau's wilderness: "A nature which I cannot put my foot through." Emerson: "We are like travelers using the cinders of a volcano to roast their eggs."

At my last sight of Peter Murray before his stabbing in the bar brawl he looked like Pinocchio in bad company, so innocent, undernourished, and flushed, his nose sharp and stark above his guileless grin.

Bon Ton potato-chip truck driver gets a blow job for $10 under my window (the price is scrawled on the wall). Tall black girl in green sweater and brown boots fluffs her thick hair as she waves him to curb, climbs partway in on the passenger side, lies on seat and pumps with her mouth for a minute or two, then quickly turns and spits out his jism. Gets out with his money in hand, scampering, prancing, very actressy, as if primed with dramatic images of herself—she's the action here on the waterfront—as she goes to hot-dog peddler with pushcart who keeps an open bottle of Coca-Cola for her to rinse her mouth with and hands her a piece of waxed paper to dry her lips on.

Molly writes ultimatums and pep talks to guinea pig and leaves them on the floor of its cage.

I see a horned owl's nest hole thirty feet up in a silver maple tree. The hole itself is owl-faced.

Mother Nature created gorillas and God made them into men, Molly says. God made the round world and Mother Nature created dinosaurs and the rest.

To draw bats you throw up a pebble and they swing toward that.

The combination of fife and drum was much more effective than either alone, and was bigger than both: the contrast conveying bravery vs. war, life vs. death.

On the Niger River, men call out from their canoes as they paddle along, and, hearing an echo, will throw a token of food overboard to the spirit there.

David Hippie's wife ate her own afterbirth after her baby was born.

Hot-natured Jersey cows eat best out-of-doors, whereas Holsteins, like the milk machines they have become, eat best standing in the barn.

Kissing my mistress, I missed my wife's scarred neck—not the actual scars of her operation, which I avoided, but the vulnerability they stood for, which touched me deeply. Smoothness seemed unsatisfying and callow.

Faulkner's Snopeses and Trollope's Slopeses.

Professional diver for Moran tugboat company stands duck-footed even without his flippers on and blinks a lot, as if punchy from the bends he has suffered, his big forehead furrowed like a pro wrestler's.

Hernia operation: "I did all the laundry but I don't have a will," I tell M. the night before. Afterward my penis turns black. And the added oddity of having a bottle of gin and a bottle of mustard hanging from two poles, linked to your veins. . . . "Better red than dead," says M. to her dermatologist as he scrapes a skin cancer off her face.

John Lennon after throwing off society's disciplines needed Yoko's.

The fine line for artists between incubation and procrastination. And there are mimickers versus explainers, "actors" versus intellects.

Writing in the present tense is like playing the harpsichord; no forte possible.

Peshka in her oxygen mask snorkeling toward death. Her lungs, when listened to through a stethoscope, sound like a day at the beach. "Am I dying? Maybe I'll make it? Maybe I'll pull through." Told not to talk, she says, "I think quite the opposite. I think I *should* talk." Dreams of drowning, or lying kidnapped with her mouth taped shut, because of the water in her lungs. Tormented by memories of World War I, when German soldiers stole her family's pots and pans to make munitions from and left a note saying "God will pay." Her job during their several flights was to "count the children." So she has awe of but no trust in God. Says, "God needs more staff." Recites a Lermontov poem, "The Runaway."

Calendars are printed now that don't even show when the moon is full.

Leonore's strangely self-indulgent yet generous gesture of clasping a lonely stranger's hand to her breast in an airport limousine, then waving good-bye to him forever.

My father guarded himself fervently against germs and chills but died prematurely of bowel cancer. Dick S.'s father guarded himself against bowel cancer by eating fruits and nuts but died by suicide, shooting himself after his car hit a rock while he was trying to drive it off the Palisades.

A mother in Little Italy puts the names of children who bother her kids in school in the freezer compartment of her refrigerator.

Nancy Miller keeps her third husband's ashes in a Cremora bottle. Dorothy Deane, dying, asked friends to put hers in their window boxes. "Café coronary" was the old name for choking on your food.

Pileated woodpeckers have survived better than ivory-billed woodpeckers; whistling swans better than trumpeters; sandhill cranes better than whooping cranes. In each case, the less complex, extravagant, exuberant birds.

Polygamous warblers have a short song, but in monogamous species the male's song is long because the monogamous female must pick a quality male who will aid her. Short song only helps a female locate a good territory where she will later fend for her young alone. Short song is thus a turf song mainly between males; long song is informative between male and a prospective female.

I see a mink crossing the road at inlet of Crystal Lake with a blackbird nestling in its teeth, a flock of redwings mobbing it, to which it is impervious. Indigo bunting eats a grasshopper, perched on a rock, with quite some difficulty with the legs. A bittern concealed behind two tussocks of grass spots a frog and twists its head back and forth, coordinating the aim of its side-looking eyes before stabbing its beak down. Grabs frog by one leg and lifts it with the frog's other leg kicking, carries it to a mud puddle beside the riverbank and spends two minutes choking it down, with many mouthfuls of water to ease the task.

Similarly, a duck will swallow a mouse with a great deal of swizzling it in the water to grease the job, and snakes lather their prey with saliva to get the meal down, lacking teeth too.

In the evening my dog barks at fireflies; also at a skunk, which stamps its feet like a boxer feinting, preparing to spray. I see scarlet tanagers and rose-breasted grosbeaks, with sweet william and rose mallow in bloom, and the mock-orange bush behind the tamaracks; raspberries a week away. Yellowthroats are nesting in the berry patch. M.'s father used to make his children smell his wrists when he came home to the apartment after working all day on skunk-fur coats. Joked of the sexual purposes these expensive coats were put to; but told her he wanted to see her getting behind the wheel of a Daimler herself some day, pulling on her "driving gloves."

The vireo and veery: high and low in a tree. Ants distribute a bloodroot's seeds. "Pale Dale" they call the local livestock dealer here, because of his slightly sinister air. "One of those sons."

Story about a heart attack victim coming home, having been told he must abstain from sex. But he must try for a child now, urgently, he feels.

The soft sigh with which a panful of steamer clams open their shells and surrender their souls.

"Life is a warning," says boxer Larry Holmes, when asked if Muhammad Ali's physical decline seems like a warning to him.

My cousin John Morley died on the Bataan Death March; M.'s cousin Seymour Mintz won the Distinguished Flying Cross for climbing onto the wing of a Flying Fortress to extinguish a fire, on one of his forty missions; then died of a heart attack at thirty-five with five children, back in New Jersey. Both of them are unsettling presences in their families.

Grandfather Morley had been paid $5 to read "the whole New Testament, every word," my mother says, when he was a boy. Grandmother Morley hired a woman to wash my mother's hair once a week, it was so long.

A good literary memoirist is often a brown-noser in life, a dissembler and hypocrite, a moth-to-power type, to have gathered the material he sells. He hid his opinions and smiled like a villain, pretended a lot.

The primly ripe mouth of a skate.

"What will become of me?" she asks, between fits of coughing. "I'm off to see the Wizard!" Going to see the cancer doctor.

"The hawk almost got me," they say in the Arctic, after a close call.

Eating deer meat: the taste of beechnuts and crab apples. A fox's bark sounds like the snort of a deer. Hunter says feeding a dog a little gunpowder in his meat makes him tough and mean.

Yoga for some is primarily athletic, for some contemplative, for others therapeutic. But light takes only a second to bounce from the moon to here.

In the early '80s poor people ate dog food in New York City, and some jet-setters wore dog collars. Short story about a woman who comes to prefer talking into people's answering machines.

Magicians have categorized five basic types of illusion: Appearance, Disappearance, Levitation, Transformation, and the Divided Woman.

For one's sex life, mine was the ideal generation. We had its mysteries in the 1950s; then got in on the sexual revolution in the 1960s and 1970s, when there was hardly such a thing as age-appropriate behavior, it seemed, and everybody mixed it up; and finally by the mid-1980s "safe sex" became the rage, which was precisely the time when we began to need safe sex because of the advent of impotence, at least situationally.

Prusten is the German term for the fluffing sound that tigers produce to talk to each other and, as it used to be, to me.

Crocodiles yawn to cool themselves in hot weather, but coyotes yawn as an agonistic device. Mice yawn from sleepiness, as people do, but we also yawn from boredom, which is to say contempt—agonistic again.

Be true to the dreams of your youth, Melville said. And when I go to the Natural History Museum at Central Park I find that I have. So many of the dioramas in the African and North American halls that awed or delighted and overwhelmed me with yearnings when I came here as a ten-year-old boy depict splendid scenes where I've managed to get since then. From Bigfoot to leopards and elephants, from the Stikine River and Alaska's fjords to Kilimanjaro and Masailand, there are quite a good many majestic intimacies pictured here in this womb-of-the-world that I have shared or achieved.

WILD THINGS

In the current happy excitement about whether we may soon discover signs of primitive life on Mars, there is a weird and tragic incongruity—because at the same time we are losing dozens of more complex but unexamined species every day right here on earth, and doing little about it. And these aren't all just the proverbial varieties of beetle with which our planet is profusely endowed. Creatures such as tigers and rhinos are also disappearing, which from childhood have been part of the furniture of our minds. Indeed, they may have helped to create our minds. When you see a lion or a tiger at the zoo, you know innately that your ancestors did too. And even if classic children's authors like Dr. Seuss and Maurice Sendak now tend to create "wild things" that are alloy animals instead of simply using the realities of a jungle, as Kipling did—Shere Khan, the tiger; Hathi, the elephant; Baloo, the bear; Kaa, the python; Bagheera, the panther—these alloy animals are surely blended from the same old veldt or jungle citizenry that shaped our imaginations to begin with and make us respond emotionally to amalgams.

I was lucky as a child because I not only had books in the house that allowed me to conceive of myself as Mowgli, Dr. Dolittle, Little Black Sambo, and other people whose lives were intertwined with those of imaginary creatures— I knew a whole spectrum of creatures myself. Living in the country, I could read *The Wind in the Willows* and encounter real toads, moles, woodchucks, muskrats, or weasels outdoors. And in 1951, at the age of eighteen, I got a job working with real tigers, elephants, monkeys, and panthers in the menagerie of the Ringling Bros. and Barnum & Bailey Circus, crossing America for fourteen dollars a week, all I wanted to eat at the cookhouse, and half of a triple-decker bunk on the first of the three trains (seventy cars) that carried the show to the next town on its nightly hops. We didn't realize then the rarity of what we were doing: that the big circus would temporarily close in 1956 and never again perform outside under canvas, and that tigers, for instance, would become desperately endangered—their ground-up vitality used as a potion for human fertility (which the world hardly needs).

We'd arrive in each town about 4:30 A.M.; the elephants and the big top on the second train two or three hours later; and then the performers around eleven. So we were on duty in a casual fashion for sixteen hours a day, interspersed with naps, or swims if the circus lot lay alongside a river, or playing with the animals. There were twenty-four Indian elephants, led by Ruth, Babe, Jewel, Modoc, and other matriarchs, plus some ninety horses. Being allergic to hay, I didn't take care of them, but delighted in trusting my life to the beneficence of those elephants, lying near their feet in the sun or walking closely between them on errands. Instead, I was assigned to care for an old chimp and a baby orangutan, a black rhinoceros, a pygmy hippo, and a gnu, a mandrill, several mangabey monkeys, the two giraffes, and a tapir. But I yearned more especially to commune with the big cats, and eventually was apprenticed to "Chief," a Mohawk Indian, who had charge of *them*. The next summer, when I came back, I found that Chief had been clawed during the Madison Square Garden engagement, had married his nurse from the hospital and stayed there in New York. Thus I had them to myself till I went back to school.

Lions are straightforward, sociable folk, easy breeders, and blessed with a humdrum, sand-colored coat that people have not wanted to strip from them and wear on their backs. Also they're lucky enough not to share a continent with the crazy Chinese, inventing mystic applications for their pulverized bones. I had a pair of lions, a maned male and a splendid female, who patiently managed to share the cramped cage, five feet by five, that Ringling Bros. provided for them. That companionship, with their bodies overlapping, seemed to calm them so much you hardly felt sorry for them, compared to our solitary, pacing tigers. I used to sleep under the lions' cage at night, if we stayed over in a large city for other performances, both because of the protection that their paws, hanging out between the bars, afforded me from wandering muggers and for the midnight music of their roars—glorious-sounding, staccato strings of roars that they exchanged as communiqués with the circus's troupe of lions who performed in the center ring under the whip of Oscar Konyot. (He was such a high-strung man, he sometimes had to stand and whip one of the side poles for a while after his act, in order to decompress.)

Tigers are more moody and unpredictable. Unlike lions, they don't form gangs or "prides," and can't be herded in the ring by somebody who knows their group dynamics and can turn the leaders and stampede them. They're more willowy and individually explosive, and must be dealt with singly, or persuaded subtly, in a sort of time-fuse confrontation. You can apply affection, but it's more a matter of slow seduction, one-on-one in the training sequence, than just becoming pals with a bunch of fractious, energetic, snarling lions. Our resident tiger trainer was a gentlemanly Englishman, Trevor Bale—not a chair-wielder in the familiar American "fighting" style of Clyde Beatty, who tried to overpower the animals instead of drawing them out, and who Konyot was imitating. The suppler, more courteous European tradition of animal training—epitomized by Alfred Court when I was a child, and by Gunther Gebel-Williams when I was middle-aged— also had had a great American practitioner, the tiger trainer Mabel Stark, who, when I saw her in California in 1953, was a quarter century past her prime and crippled by strokes but, tottering and without the use of one of her arms, still could inveigle cooperation from a cat. I was only a cageboy, not a trainer—a dreamer, not a player—but I regarded my tigers as God's cymbals when they roared and God's paint-brush when they didn't, and though of course I thought their captivity was a kind of travesty, the idea that wild tigers might not even outlive my own life span wouldn't have occurred to me.

There was a store in downtown Manhattan I used to visit, near where the banana boats came in, that sold pythons, pangolins, parrots, ocelots, tiger cubs, leopards—what couldn't you buy? And a couple of cigar stores in Times Square displayed as a sideline shrunken human heads at a hundred bucks apiece. These were the long-haired heads of Indians killed in battle, then carefully skinned off the skull and gradually steamed down to about the size of an eating-orange and stuffed to assume the proper physiognomy by Jivaro tribesmen in Ecuador, which sailors brought in from Guayaquil (though you wondered whether the middlemen weren't putting in an occasional order for more killings for the gringo market).

For all the looting of the earth's wild places, there seemed to be no end to them. The *National Geographic*, and "Bring 'em back alive" Frank Buck, and my own aspirations to be an explorer said so. My first elephant ride had been at Frank Buck's compound at the New York World's Fair in 1939, indeed. And I remember how little fuss was made one May, in 1953 or 1954, when I went backstage at the circus during its performances in Boston and two little baby tigers had just died, caged with their mother. The bosses were sorry about it (as about the cagehand who was lying in a pile of straw on the cement floor with high-fever pneumonia), but there was no sense of a significant financial or gene-pool loss. On the books—I notice from the circus's archives from the early 1950s—adult tigers were carried at a valuation of only about eleven hundred dollars apiece; a polar bear, twelve hundred; a sun bear, two hundred. Chimpanzees were about six hundred dollars; orang-utans about two thousand; and "Toto," the star-attraction gorilla, ninety-eight hundred. Giraffes were worth twenty-two hundred; cheetahs, a thousand.

Most of our cages were old army ammunition wagons from World War II, eleven feet long and partitioned so that, for instance, the two lions were housed with an enormous yolk-yellow, black-striped male Bengal tiger who must have weighed a quarter of a ton. In the tiny space allotted to him, he ignored the two lions on the other side of the dividing screen and seemed the very picture of dignified placidity, with regard to caretakers like me. Though the lions didn't ask for trouble, sprawling over each other's legs in their claustrophobic cage, they were plainly prepared to shred anybody who reached inside. They bristled and snarled like furniture scraping a floor, their handsome lips contorting into gigantic peach pits, if you had to disturb them while cleaning their cage with the long iron rod that pulled the dung out. But the tiger just lay on exhibit, stuffed unjustly into his narrow box, with an extraordinary tranquillity that was much more seductive than the bluff normalcy of the other two. In his peacefulness, he was cryptic, like a hostage king. You felt sorry for him, yet respectful: including the new workhands who had just joined the circus because they were hungry (gulping that first meal down) and wanted to sneak out of their town. And one of these neophytes, showing off for the townie girls after the afternoon show, perhaps after prodding old Joe, the ruddy-maned lion, to roar, might move the few feet on to silent, watchful Rajah, Joe's still bigger counterpart in the adjacent cage, and instead of tormenting him, might tentatively begin to pet that beautiful black-and-yellow coat through the bars, which were spaced wide enough to get even your elbow through. And—about once a year—when that young man, half-soused, did so, while the girls oohed and aahed, Rajah would wait till the hand moved up past his ribs to his magnificent shoulder, then whirl in a flash and grab and crunch it, pull the arm all the way in, rip it out of its socket and claw it entirely off.

This is not the place to itemize all the other mishaps that might befall a fourteen-dollar-a-week man, crushed by a wagon that rolled over him on the lot or tumbling off the circus train en route to somewhere at night, never to reappear. But his stump would be sewn up and he'd get a free night in the hospital, then be put on a Greyhound bus for wherever his home was, still howling in agony at every jounce.

We used to scratch the rhino's itchy cheeks, and the jaguar's risky flank, the cheetah's reluctant scalp, the hippo's willing tongue, and the four leopards' luxurious coats. It was complicated fun. Bobby, the rhino, for example, wouldn't have deliberately hurt somebody, but he didn't know his own strength when playful—or particularly care—and might inadvertently have crushed an arm against the bars in lurching about. For him, as for Chester, the large hippo (Betty Lou, the pygmy hippo, was rather unfriendly), who gaped his huge maw so that you could stick your hand in and scratch his tongue and the walls of his mouth, it was a natural procedure, akin to how the tickbirds along the Nile would have searched both their bodies for parasites. The cheetah, by contrast, growled softly, if touched—didn't like it, but probably wouldn't bite—whereas the jaguar objected with a mild rumble, and undoubtedly would have if he could have done so without bestirring himself. He was a frank, solitary animal, like the tigers but less complex than them, and a night roarer like the lions, but less bold and various in how he emitted his messages, maybe because he had no other jaguars to answer him. He was penned in a cage three and a half feet in width, alongside the cheetah's pathetically similar space (the fastest animal on earth!), with a Siberian tiger confined in the third compartment of the wagon who appeared to have gone quite mad, he was such a coiled spring of rage. Whereas the two giraffes, Edith and Boston, leaned down and licked the salt on my sweaty cheeks every hot day, the Siberian would have minced me, as he tirelessly made plain.

I believed at this point in my life that no man was complete without a parrot on his shoulder, or at least a boa constrictor looped partly over him like a friend's arm. I wasn't one of these people who think it necessary to choose between cats and dogs. I liked them both; and when I say that tigers were my first love, I mean simply sexually. I was a bad stutterer, still a virgin, could scarcely talk to other people, and felt at home in the circus partly because aberrancies were no big deal there. And we had two great big orange females compartmented in the two halves of an eleven-foot ordnance wagon who regularly, when they were in heat, presented their vulvas to me to be rubbed. So, standing at chest level with the floor of the cage, I used to reach in and gingerly do it. Chief had showed me how; and there was an ex-con who, like so many other hoboes, had materialized one day in Ohio, worked a little while, and then vanished in Indiana. The idea that caged creatures needed some solace came naturally to him. He even rubbed the old chimp's penis. What's now called "homophobia" was not a problem for him. I was bothered by that, but also by the fact that the chimpanzee was infinitely stronger than me and very disgruntled— being, after all, an individual who had been raised closely with people to perform as a cute baby in the center ring, and then abandoned to solitary confinement when he outgrew his childhood. Though he was lucky, in fact, not to have been sold for experimentation like the rest, he didn't know that, and I thought I fathomed his resentment clearly enough to steer clear of his hands and teeth, which you would be at the mercy of while masturbating him. But this fiftyish guy just out of jail went to the cage and talked to him sympathetically, when he happened to be working nearby, and reached in and massaged him a bit, like you might ease the nerves of a murderer and be in no danger, nor even ask for a cigarette in exchange afterward.

The white-ruffed, orange-and-black lady tigers, however, needed to come to the bars and swing around, squat down, and present their hind ends to be rubbed, which meant that, unlike the chimp, they weren't in a position to grab me—their mouths faced away. Then the one I was doing would stand (the other tiger in the meantime observing edgily), pace off and turn and come back and try to kill me, swiping downward with one tremendous paw extended through the bars and a roar like the crack of a landslide, bringing tears to my eyes. Knowing what was coming, I liked to step back just far enough that her paw missed me but the wind of it made my hair hop on my head, and her open mouth three feet away ended up in a deliciously subliminal snarl that she could ratchet up to motorcycle volume if she wished to. The other tiger might share her agitation briefly and chime in, and Rajah wheeled and sprayed pee around, scent-marking the ground outside of *his* cage.

Yet this was not much more furor than when tigers mate naturally. Soon she would return and squat for me to put my fingers into her vagina again; then maybe roar, swipe at me, and come to the water pan peaceably, when I slid it under the bars for her to drink from at her leisure, while I watched without giving offense, close by. I'd talk to her in her own language by making a soft chuffing sound, blowing air past my lower lip, and she answered, as zoo tigers also would, in New York or wherever I went, as long as I kept in practice. Because the secret lies in relaxing the lips, it's the opposite of a trumpeter's embouchure.

Intimacy; and I believed that I had a sixth sense. Another year, at Mabel Stark's little zoo in southern California, I climbed into a mountain lion's cage. She was another female in heat whom I had been petting through the bars. She bounded at me immediately, thrusting her paw straight into my face like a muff, but keeping her claws withdrawn.

Our four leopards—during my circus years—were utter beauties, hand-raised by the veterinarian's wife. She was an aerialist, bold, supple and strong, with white skin and black wavy hair that hung to her hips. All four loved caresses, especially Sweetheart, who was the handsomest leopard I have ever seen, with a splendid, white, breastly undercarriage and a rich, dazzling top coat, like camouflage for an empress— the mother of the rest. With her, you didn't have to be gingerly. You could simply donate your arms to her and push your face against the bars while she crouched over them, licking them like long hunks of meat with her thrillingly abrasive tongue, or else twitched her tail and purred like steady thunder as her stiff-napped, Oriental-carpet back was being scratched. Her two grown daughters milled and whirled over and about my arms and next to my face, as swift and electric as four-foot fish—the tails an extra length, lolloping up and down like puppets. The daughters purred also; and the yearling male, who was unrulier because he was beginning to shed the docility his kittenhood had trained him to, would vault around and sometimes seize my hand in his teeth and pull it as far into the cage as it would reach, without breaking my skin, but pressing down threateningly if I resisted him. Then when he had my arm under control, he flipped over on his back underneath it and in mock fashion "disemboweled" it, as if it were a gazelle that he had caught by the throat, with all four paws bicycling upward against the flesh.

But instead of destroying my arm, just like that mountain lion in California, he kept his claws in.

In East Africa, as a tourist, you watch lions from the safety of a well-roofed Land Rover, comprehending, nevertheless, as soon as a lioness stalks toward you, why early people invented spears. And you grieve for the thoughtful-looking, suffering elephants existing in shattered little herds, who have obviously witnessed so many other elephants being butchered for their ivory. Safaris are a well-oiled industry, tooled for an ever-shrinking theater of operations, but you need to reach into your mind's eye for the kind of intimations of our origins that came much more easily in Africa even twenty years ago.

When I went to southern India—flying from Nairobi to Bombay, and taking an overnight sleeper from there to Madras, in 1993—I found that wildlife viewing, like everything else, was very different in this vast disorganized democracy. As in Africa, the remnant wilderness preserves were shrinking, were strangling really, and the larger beleaguered animals knew it. But the crush and kaleidoscope of people was unlike anything I was used to. Yet it did not involve mass anarchy and the collapse of tribal certainties, or cruel politics and looming starvation, like Africa's. Democracy is invigorating.

Forty years had passed since I had been a mute young man who could speak freely only to animals and had played with Ringling Bros.' elephants and tigers. Yet though I had become more interested in people, I was still typecast as a nature writer from that early handicap and sent off to wild places to pursue old loves. In Bombay, Madras, and the newly industrial city of Coimbatore, I was lingering and lag-

ging to walk the raucous, prismatic, mysterious streets,
thereby disrupting the schedule of my local handlers, who
wanted me out of town and up in the mountain scenery as
soon as possible, where they hoped to make money from my
visit. They were travel agents—Air India had given me a free
plane ticket on the assumption that I would go up into the
Nilgiri Hills and write about sambars and sloth bears, tigers
and tahrs. If I publicized the ecotours they were projecting,
they figured that lots of rich Americans might follow me and
they could accomplish what they each aspired to do, which,
because they were young men, was either to pay for a
marriage to a Brahman or else fly to California and go hang-
gliding in the Sierras.

I was a laggard because I loved Madras, for example,
and walked or rickshawed in the streets all day, then
explored the huge iridescent crescent beach in the moonlight (though was startled to find the unmarked graves of a
few of the city's destitute underfoot at the duneline). Like
Bombay, Madras was a far less berserk, vertiginous city
than the African ones that I was familiar with. Religion, and
democracy too, were the glue. People believed in their gods
and their souls, and had the hope of the ballot. They weren't
going to crack me on the head just for a chance at my wal-
let. Indeed, in New York, a dead pauper fares much worse
than an anonymous burial on that immortal great beach,
with ridley sea turtles climbing out of the waves to lay their
eggs next to you. I found a new hatchling scrimshawing the
sand, and helped it into the sea.

The train out of Madras I'd been supposed to be on
derailed into a ravine. We went by its wreckage and stopped
for three passengers with broken arms. (In Kenya, a train
two days *after* the one I was on had crashed off a bridge into

a river, with numerous deaths.) And from Coimbatore we drove to the towns of Pollachi and Anaimalai and up into the Anaimalai Hills to a high old British logging camp called Top Slip because the teakwood and rosewood had been slid downhill from there, but which is now the Indira Gandhi Wildlife Sanctuary, though with the aid of elephants it's still being partially logged. The hushed, handsome, rising and plunging forest had a panoply of birds—golden orioles, scarlet minivets, racquet-tailed drongos, pretty "dollar birds," and crow pheasants, green barbets, blue-winged parakeets, blossom-headed woodpeckers, and mynah birds. We saw these, and tahrs (an endangered wild goat) and sambars (a large dark form of deer), big bison, and wild boars, a black-and-white porcupine, mongooses and civets, green parrots, magpies, hoopoes, hornbills, plentiful chital deer, red with white spots, and flamboyantly plumaged jungle fowl, langur monkeys, macaques, mouse-deer holes, and a nine-colored pitta bird.

I was traveling at this stage with Salim, a young university-educated Shiite Muslim from Madras. His father was a travel agent posted to Abu Dhabi, his mother a Hindu, his early schooling Catholic. His first language had been English because his father otherwise spoke Urdu. Our local guide, Sabrimathu, was about seventy years old and what is called in India a "tribal," meaning from one of the fragile indigenous tribes, the Kadar. Despite a few protections the government gives them (analogous to the position of American Indians), they tend to miss the British when you talk to them, because the British praised and encouraged their tracking skills. In the present money or bureaucratic economy, with a seething agglomeration of subcontinental humanity everywhere, they are at best an afterthought, like an eccentric, illiterate great-uncle in a ragged dhoti marooned in the attic. Sabrimathu carried a little sack of tobacco leaves to chew, and a bush knife; and like the British, I was delighted to listen to him communicate with another Kadar man on the opposite hillside by means of langur barks, regarding the whereabouts of a dozen elephants we were following. We broke off hastily when the other man let us know they had a baby with them.

Originally, Sabrimathu said, two peoples had inhabited these high woods. The Kadar carried spears and lived by gathering small creatures and forest plants, or scavenging from red-dog (dhole) kills, if they could surround the pack and drive them off. With brands from a campfire as weapons and windfall shelters, they could coexist with the forest's tigers and also the bison, which are like the African buffalo. But there was no way to stand up to the elephants. They'd had to hide, run and hide, abandon any permanent settlement that the elephants approached. The other tribe, the Kurumbas, used bows and arrows to hunt with, shooting birds out of the trees for food and skirmishing with Sabrimathu's group, whose language they didn't speak. They, too, fled the elephants when a playful herd or a rogue bull in "musth" rampaged through, but feared the teak loggers and the British more, and so vanished north.

Sabrimathu's group numbers only a few hundred now, in ten or fifteen tiny communities of thatch huts, on this rugged borderland between the Cochin district of the state of Kerala and Tamil Nadu, where I'd come from. He had a confiding face, unkempt gray hair, a woodsman's elastic sense of time, and a blurry sort of shuffling manner by which he tried to elide and conceal his feelings when supervisors and clerks condescended to him. Of course, on the contrary, I was all ears, like the British naturalists and tiger hunters who had formerly employed his skills, or the World Wildlife Fund researcher he said he'd caught a long python for and put it in a burlap sack. He pointed up a forest stream to where the pythons bred; and later pointed at a knot of crags under a cliff of the Perunkundru Hills, where a leopard mother retreated each year to bear her kits; and to a distant thicket of sidehill evergreens where a tiger generally did the same. Up on a bare saddle of scree, a bit of footpath was visible where he had met a tiger coming toward him—that situation where, he said, you "just stand still and see whether your time has come." It hadn't, though once a tiger jumped at him in the underbrush when he was helping a forestry official track a man-eater. It missed. He was injured another time, when he surprised a bison on a narrow trail and it charged and knocked him out and horned his arm; he showed me the scars, healed by forest medicines.

The British had naturally encouraged the Kadar people to become the mahouts here, capturing and training the local wild elephants—which they tentatively did, overcoming their age-old fears. I remember hearing, in northern Canada and Alaska, how the New World Indians at first had been unsatisfactory guides on grizzly-hunting expeditions because even though they might be wizards at tracking grizzlies, having practiced for thousands of years equipped with "stone-age" weapons, their purpose in doing so was mainly to avoid the beasts. They were so fearful that newcomers—white bullyboys with fat-caliber rifles—still made fun of them. But here, in this other kind of devouring, homogenizing democracy, it was not the raj or later visiting whites but other Indians who made difficulties. And about twenty years after independence, Sabrimathu's remnant tribe, so fragile

anyway in the new India, had been ousted from their livelihood as elephant handlers by a new people: cattle herders,
more adaptable and sophisticated, the Pulasaris, who came
up from the plains—at first two families, then more. After
apprenticing with the Kadar, the Pulasaris had finagled or
genuinely convinced the authorities that they would be
better at doing it.

We stopped at their camp, located beside a boisterous
small river, the Varagalear, in a cut between hills in the deep
lovely woods, where they earn about sixty dollars a month,
three times a laborer's wage, for working a dozen elephants.
We arrived in the evening as the usurpers were finishing
washing the beasts, and they jeered at poor Sabrimathu's
chagrin as they showed us a five-year-old they were training
to blow on a harmonica, lift one of her feet with her trunk,
and cover one eye with her ear. She lay down in the swirling
warm stream with only her trunk raised above the current to
breathe, while the foreman washed her tusks, lips, and eye-
lids. The others were not as tame, and after being watered,
washed, and fed, were chained for the night, though the wild
herd kept close tabs on them from nearby and sometimes
came down in the night and mingled with them.

The several families of interlopers had small children, and
it was idyllic, with the foaming creek and the rushing wind in
the trees, miles from another human sound, yet protected
from any wandering tiger by the throng of elephants, swaying
on their rhythmic feet and swinging their idiosyncratic trunks
to private tempos. I remembered feeling this safe in the circus, sleeping under the big cats' cages, knowing that any
mugger who crept up on me would provoke a roar that would
stop his heart, or if he swung a little bit wide in the dark, he'd
encounter the row of elephants, who would step on him.

Naturally I wanted to see a tiger, though there wasn't much chance of that. We drove to a few overlooks where they occasionally were sighted on a beach of the stream below, but didn't walk anywhere after dark. An old Kadar man with prostate problems had been seized in Sabrimathu's little hamlet the year before, when he needed to pee in the middle of the night and left his hut. But the same villagers went out in the woods every day, gathering teak seeds from the forest floor to sell, or honey and beeswax from clefts in cliffs and hollow trees, or sago, cardamom, ginger. Or they collected soap nuts for making shampoo, or guided the Forestry Service men on inspection tours, in order to obtain the rice that had become their new staff of life and didn't grow here. They also used to catch civets for the perfume industry, and had guided tiger-rug hunters, but these latter ventures were now illegal and what poaching went on was done by gangs of in-and-out thugs with connections to outside smugglers, not by naive tribal people. Sabrimathu reminded me of various aged Eskimos, American Indians, and African subsistence hunters I've met too briefly over the years, who, like him, knew a thousand specifics no one will know at all when they are gone, though nobody they had any contact with seemed to care much now about what they knew. They too lived wind-scented, sunlit, star-soaked, spirit-shot lives. Humble on one level, proud on another, Sabrimathu was vulnerable to exploitation and insult partly just because he was so tactile and open to everything else. Like those millions of American Indians who disappeared way before their time, he was rooted in place. He could be chopped like a tree or shot like a songbird.

Early on our last day at Top Slip, I woke Salim—my young travel-agent, biology-major, Muslim-Hindu-Christian escort—and told him I'd like to go on a bird walk. Amenable though sleepy, he drove me ten miles downhill through the woods to Thunnakadu Reservoir, which is a pretty lake that was created in 1967 and looks perhaps four miles long. The valley it drowned is also lovely, set between protected bands of forest highlands of the Cardomon Hills and flowing toward the Malabar coastline on the Arabian Sea. The road we traveled gets only one bus a day, and at the lake there was no settlement at all except half a dozen wooden cabins for the road crew. They were still asleep, so we simply walked across the top of the dam to the wild side of the lake, as the fragrant, misty blues of dawn were broken by the strong-slanting yellow sun. Cormorants and kingfishers were diving, and pond herons prowling the bank, and we saw a fishing eagle. There was a bamboo raft tied ashore, of the sort the Kadar use to go angling for armlength larder fish that they can dry. Salim's knowledge of the birds we heard and saw was that of a practical-minded young man of many interests. He was impatient with India's religious sectarianism, and rather favorable toward the social changes that the brave women's movement in big cities such as Madras were aiming for. He'd traveled some, and wanted to travel more, and so the antiquarian curiosity that foreign tourists like me displayed was not of much interest to him. He said, for instance, when I asked, that, yes, Gandhi's example was still remembered in India, not ignored, but not followed either. A modern capitalist, commonsense democracy was what he wanted, with money, decency, mobility.

We walked and chatted on a footpath along the lake, while red-wattled lapwings, the "policemen of the forest," kept noisy watch over our progress, along with several "babblers," the "seven sisters" birds, so called because they always move in a group. A big Brahminy kite, white-headed but otherwise a beautiful orangey brown, was being hassled by a bunch of crows above the trees, much as birds of prey are in the United States. We saw a leopard's precise tracks, and then a largish tiger's sprawling pugs, and four bear feces, berry-filled, in different stages of drying out, as if this path was a thoroughfare. Though Salim had never seen a leopard or a tiger, he was in favor of turning back, yet not insistently so. There was no disputing what we were looking at—the tiger and the bear could have been nothing else—yet, after all, we could have expected that these animals would come down to drink and forage a bit at night, before climbing the bluff behind the lake again.

Overhead, a troop of langur monkeys swinging in the branches had begun to whoop the alarm. It had been quiet except for the bird calls at dawn and sunrise and a few magpie and lapwing minatory cries. But entering this neck of the woods provoked a monkey cacophony, a real hollering that seemed part fearful bark or howl and part self-important fun—a rather gay razzing once they were accustomed to us and had done their primary job. We continued our stroll for another quarter mile, occasioning lots of hubbub because each marginal youngster had to prove that he knew his duty too, not just the sentinels and the leaders. But then there was an added note, deeper in pitch, exasperated and abrupt. The langurs' hullabaloo at first had masked it, or the fact that with our presence so much advertised, we had now felt free to gab in normal tones, and therefore heard the gravelly, landslide-sounding rumble a little ahead of us as just perhaps some sort of patriarchal intervention from within the monkey clan—not superimposed.

We kept walking. It was repeated. Not only bigger lungs and a lower pitch: The temper of the roar was totally different, like a combat colonel interrupting the chatter of a bunch of hyperexcited privates. Rajah had roared horrendously at me a few times when I had been hosing his cage or cleaning it with the long iron rod and had bumped him inadvertently. And from a distance of forty years, those capsizing blasts reverberated for me.

"That's not a monkey!" Salim and I said simultaneously. Then, in about the time that a double-take takes, "Isn't that a tiger?" We each nodded and smiled—then after three or four steps, stopped in our tracks. The lake was on our left and the woods extended to the bluff, a few hundred feet high to the right, which was one reason why a nettled tiger, too, might feel he had been hemmed in. That he had roared at us, instead of waiting silently in the undergrowth beside the trail to simply kill us, was a good sign. On the other hand, he could have withdrawn up the valley, or a hundred yards to the side, without our ever knowing about him. He or she was obviously not doing that. Was he lying on a kill? Or was she a lady with some half-grown cubs? The roars, instead of ceasing when we turned around and started walking back toward the area of the dam, now redoubled in exasperation, as if the tiger, like the two caged females I'd masturbated in the circus, had flown into a sudden, unreasonable rage. Furthermore (from the volume and tone, I guessed he was male), he was now paralleling us, maybe forty or fifty yards in—not visible, but roaring repeatedly, not letting us depart without a terrific chastening. He could have cut us off and mauled us, or driven us into the lake, but didn't; and eventually we met four Kadar men in dhotis who were collecting teak seeds and told them about him. Like us, they turned around immediately and fled at an inconspicuously quick scuttle.

The crew chief, when we got back to the road, said in Tamil to Salim, "Oh, you shouldn't have gone there. That side of the lake is where the tiger lives." The estimate of the wildlife warden at headquarters was a census of thirty-five in these seven hundred square miles.

Being a fan of adages such as "a stitch in time," "an apple a day," "turnabout is fair play" or "what goes around comes around," I was pleased by the symmetry of an old tiger cageboy like me who had tried to be superkind being spared in India forty years later. As in grizzly country, I was glad, too, that it was still possible to experience a fright from a wilderness creature. In this Tamil Nadu region in 1993, one didn't hear talk yet of tigers being poached for the Chinese aphrodisiac market—only elephants for their tusks and sandalwood for its scented properties. But there are close to a billion people in India, and scarcely two thousand tigers. And since Indira Gandhi had decided that tigers ought to be protected, a number of generations have grown up that are less afraid of people, at the same time as the territory available for them to roam in is being constricted from every side. Like grizzlies, the point about tigers is that from our standpoint they are unpredictable. They fly off the handle when pressured, and need more than just a specified number of square miles to provide a food source or enough prey animals. Like the Kadar, they are elastic in their sense of time. They need space for their whims and passions and shifts of emotions. They weave more as they walk.

An Australian orthopedist had turned up at Top Slip after lecturing at a conference in Coimbatore, instructing the local doctors in how to handle broken backs—a commonplace where people climb coconut trees. But the hospitals were full of people with lung ailments from the dust that was everywhere, he said, or who'd gotten busted in road crashes.

We drove back down from these rosewood, teak, and tamarind forests to Anaimalai and Pollachi, and then to Mettuppalaiyam, in several hours of the wildest riding I've ever experienced. It's a nation where huge painted diesel lorries and long blue buses career at dizzying speed past countless oxcarts, hundreds of bicyclists, and thousands of pedestrians on jerry-built highways through continuous strings of makeshift villages. Not, however, merely like Africa, because of this quintupled congestion of people walking and crossing against the tenfold vehicular and animal traffic: cattle, goats, donkeys, and camels, jalopies, pickups, taxi-vans, swarming scooters, mopeds, occasional tractors, and hosts of schoolchildren, urchins, waifs, toddlers, and folks struggling on canes and crutches. And it's not so much that you fear dying (that the bullock with red-painted horns, struck broadside, will do you in) as that some of these confident, innocent citizens going about their business—hour by hour, more individual humanity in puce and aquamarine saris at instant risk than you have seen anywhere else in the world—are going to get smashed up into the air or crushed under the tires. Little unattended kids, grumpy old men strutting along because of their back and leg ailments, mammas shopping purposefully for beans and sunflower seeds from vociferous peddlers, customers at stand-up tea shops half-forced out in the traffic, or wedding parties at colorful, compact temples of stone and plaster likewise spilling outside. The many schoolyards debouched into the street, plus dozens of markets constructed of stucco and low-slung canvas. And many people, to save rupees, were walking for miles with only a rudimentary familiarity with the dangers that motor vehicles can pose. Nor were the drivers' skills uniform. Obtaining a license was not so much taking a test as paying a bribe, and the road often whittled down to a single lane.

We whizzed along at velocities approaching airplane speed, with corkscrew, brake-slamming maneuvers, for several hours, stopping one time for rice, fried fish, and tea; then slept overnight in Mettuppalaiyam at a hotel with fleas, before boarding a narrow-gauge railway train in the dark of the morning to go thirty miles up to the resort town of Udagamandalam, or "Ooty," as it's called, where British colonials are said to have invented snooker at the Ooty Club. Mettuppalaiyam, though, is a paper-company city where a siren awoke everybody at six A.M. for the shift change—eucalyptus plantations all around provide the pulp.

Nevertheless, the clip-clop of steel-shod oxen on the pavement was constant; and the all-night, dimly lurid-looking orange neon lighting was reminiscent of the 1930s in America. So was the hunger. Whereas in Africa I had seen people who were literally starving to skin and bones (and other people knocked dead on the highway in much sparser traffic because they were even less used to cars), the hunger that I saw in India, whether in Bombay, Madras, Coimbatore, or Mettuppalaiyam, was like missed-meals nutrition during the Depression in America. As I waited for this train, for instance, I was eating a banana on the platform. I'd half-finished it when a group of schoolgirls came along, perhaps twelve years old, neatly dressed in their uniforms. They looked presentable, conventional, not "untouchable," and one, a bit more confident, reached out tentatively toward my banana. "May I?" When of course I handed it to her, she immediately wolfed it down, as two other girls tried to grab it away. It may have been her only breakfast, but in Africa I had seen girls and boys of the same age in rags in a war zone who hadn't eaten in a couple of weeks. And in America in the 1990s, by contrast, if you offered a half-eaten banana to a beggar on the street, you might be wiping spittle off your face.

The vegetarian politeness and busy energies of so many of India's famous personalities make the place seem more channeled than it actually is. One forgot that both Indira Gandhi, and then her son Rajiv Gandhi, when he took over the prime ministership, had been assassinated—the latter near Madras in 1991; I visited the spot—not to mention *the* Gandhi, before that. And when I'd arrived at Bombay's airport, I didn't realize that an estimated four thousand people, primarily Muslims, had recently been killed in sectarian rioting in that city alone. I was apprehensive enough to be landing alone with no reservations in a strange country at 3:00 A.M., but noticed my Sikh taxi driver was semihysterical. It turned out that he'd been waiting at the airport for nineteen hours for a fare, and this because it was the safest place to hide. All of the Sikh or Muslim cabbies, he said, had fled there. Yet I soon went around to visit the hanging gardens, a Jain temple, Mahatma Gandhi's house, the Prince of Wales Museum, the aquarium with triggerfish and eagle rays, the island of the Elephant Caves, the monumental arched Gateway of India that the British built in 1927 at the port, and other stuff, like any charmed-life tourist.

Ooty is up at 7,500 feet, twice as high as Top Slip, and by paying a couple of dollars in baksheesh I got to ride in the little blue-and-red, coal-fired engine with a gazelle painted on the side that was pushing the ramshackle five-car train. We rode through sugarcane and rice fields and mango-fruit and betel-nut plantations; saw mushroom farms and truck gardens for carrots, beans, and potatoes, plus coffee and cinchona (quinine) production. The engine gripped the grades, belching white steam and black smoke (*I-think-I-can, I-think-I-can*). Roses bloomed in the cuts, between dark tunnels and white cataracts. We had trekkers from Europe doing their walkabouts, and a bunch of army recruits whom we dropped at a training base at Wellington halfway up, and two elderly Canadians. The man, a civil engineer in far-off spots like this, had never married till his sixties, but had once adopted four orphans as foster children here, and was now revisiting them all to see if they belonged in his will, as he told me later at the Southern Star Hotel.

I-thought-I-could, I-thought-I-could, the little cog train began to say. The fireman dropped off lumps of coal for poor women (I assumed, unless they were his relatives) who gathered at hidden nooks along our route. The coffee fields had been lower down. At cooler altitudes were green-tea plantations, for which the Nilgiris, or Blue Hills, are famous. But there were also long green ravines and thickly forested tangents extending down the mountainside that contained fragments of the holy forest of original wild vegetation, as complex as Creation, that are called *sholas* and preserve God's own infinitely harmonious unruliness. At least in southern India, when you visit a temple you may find parrots nesting in the walls, monkeys perched on the turrets, and a cobra coiled in the quietest of the recesses. Similarly, an uncut forest is regarded as having some magic, perhaps a reservoir of the godhead. It is going to get cut, but it is also loved.

Ooty, "Queen of the Hill Stations," is a spacious, vaguely rakish, prosperous little city with film and fertilizer factories, assorted tasty eateries, and shops and hotels. Too quickly, we left in a 1977 Willys Jeep named Theena on a drive of several bumpy hours to an isolated trekkers' cabin at Mukkurthi Reservoir, because my mission, courtesy of the Indian government, was still to see some wild places. Salim, my dark-browed, acned, saturnine, big-featured, practical-minded, Shiite-Hindu-Christian, biology-major guide from the metropolis of Madras had handed me over to a new guy. Habib was a sunnier Ooty man from a tea-growing family, with a business degree. He was a Sunni Muslim who loved to hike and hang-glide, as well as the good life otherwise, and hoped that whatever I wrote would draw enough Californians to Ooty that he could use his money from "inbound tourism" to enable him to travel to California himself, where he wanted to hang out in the Bay Area just as much as an American might wish to come here. Habib was a handsome outdoorsman with an eye for the majesty of nature, a curiosity about history, and sympathy for the aboriginal peoples still left around. Like Salim—who was linked a bit with university life in Madras, and had put me in touch with a few of its activist idealists, without wishing to be one—Habib was quite an interesting man. In fact, he'd deserted his middle-class background and gone off to live in a three-family village of Toda herdsmen in a place called Parson's Valley, after falling in love with a Toda girl, for half a year. On one of his hikes last month, he had crouched in a hollow and watched two mating tigers climb past him toward these high grass hills where we were now—the epitome of harassed, focused wildness, he said, though splendidly colored—red, white, black, orange, and yellow.

And the national Electricity Board had caused half a dozen finger lakes to be created for hydroelectric purposes, supplying power plants downriver at Paikara. Overlogging and a drought had then scoured and eroded the slopes brown. But small ragged crews of men, camped in lean-tos, were replanting, putting in fast-growing acacia seedlings that could be cut for firewood or wattles for hut-building to truck to the city in a few years. (You *must* believe that human beings are a good idea to like India. Everything is people, people, people, but without the vaunting religious assumptions of human superiority of the West.)

I walked several miles at sunrise, encountering fifteen gray-black bison coming off the mountain for a morning drink, before I turned back. We rightly feared each other; I'm sure my heart beat just as fast as theirs. At intervals, a winding creekbed a hundred yards wide had been permitted to keep its tall, tangled *shola* trees and undergrowth, and this is where the whooping black monkeys that I now heard and other wildlife hid—the deer, the elephants, the "white panthers," and "black panthers" that the caretaker at our cabin, Gopal, and his wife, Agniesh, described. They were old folk from Mysore who had gone north and worked at a hotel at the Taj Mahal for a while, being used to Europeans, but had returned here, where thirty years ago Gopal had guided British hunters on horseback after tigers, elephants, tahr, bison, sambar, and chital, with a pack of thirty-six hounds specially trained for the pursuit of different quarry. He was paid a hundred rupees whenever they killed a tiger, at a time when a laborer's monthly wage was fifteen rupees. Now he just watches through the window when a tiger strides by on the jeep track outside and, if it's rutting, stops and paces and sprays pee and chuffs at him. His young son,

Aiyappan (named for a god who can take human form), walks back and forth to Ooty every week to school. This is, incidentally, the territory where the children's story *Little Black Sambo* was written.

We gave Aiyappan a lift. The rolling landscape, even largely stripped of trees, retained an exhilarating sweep way off to the far horizon, where the biggest mountaintop still represented the Todas' afterlife, Habib said, a site where the living tribespeople made an effort to visit the spirits of their ancestors at certain intervals—though like all their less convenient customs, this one was under siege. Not many Todas were still observant enough to undertake a hundred-mile walk for such an ancient purpose. But just the lunging terrain can seem to speak exultantly at a distance, as it goes sailing over lakes, blue gulfs, and mystery forests, up toward the drifting clouds.

It was Sunday. Back in Ooty, the cart horses had been turned loose for the day. The week's washing was spread in Brobdingnagian proportions across a whole vacant field near the public faucets, and the roadside tea houses were cheerfully crowded. A Communist hammer and sickle had been chalked on one of the buildings. A little beyond that, a dozen green quarter-moon flags were flying from a tin hovel, alongside a loudspeaker horn for praising Allah. Further on, nestled in a lusher garden, stood a Hindu temple decorated with a sculpture of Ganesha, the elephant-headed, potbellied god, riding on a rat, and other emblems and effigies. We drove to the top of Dodabetta, at 8,700 feet the highest mountain in the Nilgiris. It's cold and bouldery and wild up there in spite of the excursion road that has been built, and formidable creatures like leopards and tigers come out at night—though one might repeat that in this part of India, nature shares at least symbolic full citizenship with humanity. Each may be mistreated, but people are part of nature, not a biblically sanctioned master race.

Habib said his Toda girlfriend had married another man after he broke up with her. Although she continued to live in her home village, she commuted by bus to a job as a lab technician in Coonoor, making rabies vaccine. The Todas, when they adapt to contemporary conditions, tend to do pretty well, he said, though only about seven hundred and fifty are left in the world. Because of their reputation for integrity they may be hired to manage a tea plantation, for instance. The ones who stay in the traditional settlements of four or five stone-and-mud, wattle-and-grass-roofed huts in a cluster on a hilltop are rather demoralized, however. For one thing, they'd always fermented their own home brew, but now alcohol comes too strong, too available, from the store; and the people who surround them in numbing majorities, like the Badagas, or the various outlanders and flatlanders who have migrated in, are swamping the Todas.

After a night's sleep in Ooty, we drove out to Bigupathimund Camp, which is high up in the mountains, near the head of two lively streams, with forests all around, but also a far-flung view—one of Habib's favorite spots. The four Toda families who lived in a small mud-walled compound there knew his friendly interest to be sincere and so welcomed us. The government gives each Toda man five acres to farm when he marries, so they had a fine moist little saddle of the mountaintop under cultivation, thick with carrots and onions, though wild boars and bears occasionally marauded through. I heard shouts all night, and a large animal rushing by our shelter once in the dark. Next morning they asked if I had a gun, because of one particular wild pig that sticks and stones and hollering couldn't deter. A leopard, too, had been around, but no tigers for a year or so.

We were staying in a rest house that the British had built. The Todas are tall, rather light-skinned or coffee-colored, and have Aryanish, delicate features. But because they are vegetarians and stay-at-homes, they were not used much as hunting guides by the British officers who vacationed here. Indeed, the Badaga watchman at our house offered to procure us a bunch of prostitutes from his village three miles downhill at about a dollar apiece for the night— as he said he often did for Forestry officials and other guests. The Todas complained of the noise and atmosphere of debauchery inflicted on them by these revels. Such a tiny remnant, really, on a small reserve, they had a much more serious problem, too. They'd just suffered the loss of their sacred buffalo, which had been stolen from the precincts of the temple nearby in the woods that they had maintained, they told me, for at least two hundred years. And she could not simply be replaced by buying a water buffalo in the marketplace, because a temple buffalo must be descended from another temple buffalo. Definitively, she must also be able to roam free in the *shola*, going and coming whenever she wishes, not penned up, and therefore would now be at risk, in this jammed and polyglot, impious age, of being grabbed and butchered for food by people of other allegiances, or simply captured and led on a rope to some faraway market for sale. Their ordinary buffaloes also roamed free, but the calves were kept at the settlement so that the mothers would return at night, whereas this one temple buffalo is always supposed to be totally free, keep her calf where she wishes, and live in the forest, not in camp.

So, they were in anguish over the unknown fate of this sacred, very personable, particular buffalo. They are a *buffalo people*, and by chance we had arrived at a point, February 15, when they were planning to go and rededicate their temple—one of only two active temples that all of the Todas had (a third having fallen into disuse). They wished to try to reverse a long sequence of bad luck, and pray for the buffalo's welfare, and ask that she be taken care of, wherever she was. Their other domestic animals, mainly cattle but a few buffalo, numbered less than twenty, anyway, and this band was so vulnerably small that when they held a dance for us the next evening by firelight in the little mud compound of four houses, only two men and five women performed—singing and shuffling in a swaying, rotating circle, with four kids watching. An old man blew the two-foot bamboo flute. This was blackened and sounded a bit like a piccolo; then when he hung a tin cup on the end to alter its tone, like an oboe.

Our host, as Habib spelled his name, was M'Thekalmudi, a thin-mustached man whose face looked like Joe DiMaggio's and who gave his age as forty-nine and his wife's age as twenty-seven. Three of the kids were theirs and the other his younger brother's. The women could have nothing at all to do with the rituals of the temple, but otherwise seemed rather equal and free, though they did perform a periodic ritual of obeisance to a husband or elder man, kneeling and placing his foot on their heads. But some Hindu women do that as well. Everybody gradually got happier, in dancing. Yet M'Thekalmudi confessed in his language with some foreboding that even the flute "didn't sound right."

M'Thekalmudi's wife brought me a ceremonious cup of buffalo milk, had me remove my shoes, and let me squeeze into her house, which was loaf-shaped, with a low, rounded roof. Half the horizontal space was taken up by a sleeping platform made of boards and dried dung. The small door was also wooden and could be locked—small doors discourage animals, wild or tame, from coming inside. There were no windows, but several oil lamps set on niches or shelves, and a mud fireplace with a rack for firewood and a smoke hole going out. Wood and bamboo had been used to frame the mud walls, and there were mattocks hanging from the rafters, and buffalo-horn-shaped tree branches, religious in nature, plus a few framed family pictures tacked up. At the back wall were shelves for clothes and food in storage vessels, and on the floor, several stainless steel pots that contained water. It was smoky but cozy—my hostess gracefully communicating in sign language—and the next day I saw her sister and her lugging pails of cows' milk down the hill toward the Badaga village to sell for cash, a six-mile round-trip. The buffaloes' milk was always kept separate. The Kota tribe were also neighbors of the Todas, and furnished them with pottery and bush knives in exchange for milk, or perhaps for meat when a cow died, or when a male buffalo was sacrificed after a man had died—because the Todas did not eat meat, just left it in the forest for the Kotas or hyenas or whomever.

In the morning the men prayed in a short, low, windowless, grass-roofed, barrel-curved minor temple, built of wood and fitted slabs of stone, that was located right in the village, as they did every day—not a place that even Habib could venture inside—after the rituals of milking their buffaloes and smearing some buffalo cream in their hair. An upright stone slab stood in front, and also two large round stones in the village's council area. A boy must be able to lift one of these, stand up, and hurl it over his shoulder before he married and became a man.

Habib said he'd left his girlfriend's Toda family after six months or so because the routine of lazing on a hillside watching their seven cows graze all day long finally became boring, though he'd liked the purity of it. Now he watched his own family's ten acres of tea shrubs grow. I teased him when he said he was religious, asking him if he wouldn't rather make a pilgrimage to Mecca than go hang-glide in California after the tourists began paying him to bring them here. He said Mecca, yes, but not as much as California.

Then we accompanied the men on their poignant trip to the central temple, a humble walk through field and forest of a couple of miles. Eight Toda men and two boys were involved, which—for such a powerful occasion—was all the more affecting; and when we got close we took our footwear off. Through Habib, M'Thekalmudi said, "We all used to be healthy. Could run up any mountain and not have to stop. But now we don't exert ourselves." Everyone had abstained from sex last night after the dance and had fasted this morning. They wore no western clothes; instead they had on white cotton dhotis and the knitted buffalo-wool shawls that their wives make for them, which take four months apiece.

Traditionally, the men would have spent January alone at this temple, living only on rice and milk from the temple buffalo, neither smoking, drinking, nor visiting women. But they hadn't this year because of the stolen buffalo. We stopped first at a whetstone pool of clean spring water (it was lined with whetstones you could sharpen your bush knife on). Here everybody bathed once again, though they had done so in the village too, and put sandalwood powder in dots on their foreheads.

We approached the temple in attentive anticipation, and my unspoken worry that it might seem anticlimactic proved needless. It stood in a riveting cup-shaped grotto, noisy with bird and monkey calls, in a sumptuous, unspoiled forest. It was conical, very lofty and exceptional-looking, grass-roofed, with a siding of bamboo withes bound together and overlaid with more grass, except for the bottom five feet, which was constructed of upright stone slabs that the grass overhung. I would guess it was thirty-five feet high, altogether. Inside, I was told, five twelve-foot stone pillars lent additional support, and some much taller teepee-style treeposts. Inset in the front was a gnomish round stone door, with a buffalo skull fastened over it, and other wood and metal emblems. In a half circle outside were several concentric stone walls and, between them, a slender stone slab. Behind the temple was a comely huge "temple tree." But they let nature choose the species that it would be. And another large tree stood in front, though this one had been vandalized by intruders with graffiti. Nearby was a three-foot stone upon which, until about a hundred years ago, a naked man, chosen from a different village each year, used to sit fasting for fifteen days, except for the buffalo butter poured over him every third of those days—"shortening his own life for the glory of God."

Of course the soul of the whole place should have been the temple buffalo, free-roaming, divinely descended, ultimately from the original Buffalo given to mankind at the Buffalo Tree. M'Thekalmudi sent a runner several miles to that very tree of life to bring me a peeled foot-length sprig, which in itself formed horns like a buffalo's. He said they come here, however, for both deaths and festivals; "any good or bad."

They knelt and prayed in unison for a time, led by an older man. And we saw, on our leisurely walk back to the hamlet of Bigupathimund, a large gray stone which was a woman who (even though it wasn't her fault) had passed too close to the temple. She'd been sick, and her brothers, in carrying her home on a litter, had taken the shortest route, and she was turned to stone in an utter instant.

"If you do wrong," M'Thekalmudi added, speaking of the present, "God will lead the tiger straight to you in the woods."

We also saw "the leap of joy," an incredible jump marked by two black stones that was once made by a man of legend, returning from a journey, when he was told that both his previously barren wife and his buffalo had given birth to babies. He had a sack of grain on his shoulders at the time, so if you try to duplicate his jump, you should too.

And, crossing a ford of the stream, we saw where the sun once entered the earth for a brief spell and the world went dark, after two Toda villages had been quarreling about who "owned" the stream. "The temple brought the sun down," M'Thekalmudi said. And now the figure of a praying god is gradually rising from a rock in the middle of the water—hands together, and with a helmet head like an astronaut's—a little more every year.

One of the men, walking down to the valley for cigarettes after the ceremony, saw a leopard and then a bear along the stream. He told me they have a special calming sound that they utter from the belly, when they encounter an elephant deep in the woods, so the elephant thinks, *Oh, that's just a Toda.*

We left the Todas, and drove for several hours out of the high country, through tea and cinchona plantations, to Kotagiri, and down to the Moyar River Valley, then wound up that into another sizable forest preserve, and finally traveled another twenty unpopulated miles to a town called Thengumarahda, reachable from the end of the dirt road only by boarding a coracle, a circular little buffalo-hide skinboat, and then walking across a mile of rice and peanut fields. A mountain called Kodanad loomed overhead, with many cliffs and draws and stringy waterfalls and other visible complexities. To climb down to Thengumarahda from the road on top of Kodanad took five hours, if you didn't lose your way, Habib said.

The rice had just been cut with scythes. Wheeling lines of oxen, five abreast, were trampling it to separate the grains from the grass, which would later be fed to the animals as hay, and the grain then tossed in screens by groups of women to separate the chaff. The peanuts were planted in alternation, as nitrogen-rich legumes. All told, three or four crops a year were fitted in. Though sugarcane might have been more profitable, the wild elephants found sugar juice irresistible and would come stomping into the fields after it at night. They sometimes broke down banana trees, too, to get the fruit, and the watchmen would throw firecrackers or firebrands at them. But the banana orchards they'd damage were not so extensive. Coconuts were an elephant-proof crop, as well as limes, and there were little plots of mulberries, chili peppers, betel nuts, and whatnot.

Thengumarahda had been established as a Gandhian agricultural cooperative of a hundred and fifty families on five hundred acres at the time of independence in 1947, Habib said, and was the only one of maybe forty of these idealistic projects in India that had survived. Factionalism, greed, debauchery, and "free enterprise" had brought the others down.

I wasn't functioning as a journalist checking facts on this brief tour, however. Rather, I was listening to the ancient music I was hearing: like how they bang two pans together if a tiger comes. We were situated again in a former British rest house used by the Forestry Service. A bare, tiled-floor, whitewashed structure at the edge of the village, it had a splendid view of the ramparts of Mount Konadad going up two or three thousand feet, with a lot of forest in between and half a dozen wooded pocket sanctuaries to gaze at higher up, ideal denning places for a hyena family or a mamma bear or big cat or an old elephant that just wanted to be off by himself. In India the ivory poaching has decimated only the males, because female Indian elephants (unlike their African counterparts) do not have tusks. So what you have are herds of angry females who have witnessed a number of cruel, treacherous, lingering deaths of bulls that they've known well—shot from ambush—whose tusks were then hacked off. The smugglers' ("bandits") trail was pointed out to me, in fact.

If chased by an elephant, you run in a zigzag, hide, and dash away when discovered, hide again and dash if rediscovered, then turn suddenly, and turn again, because an elephant, though fast in a straight line, is less maneuverable than you are. It will stop and listen for you, raising its trunk to sniff the air, sometimes pawing one foot, and spread its ears "like a cobra's hood." It can push down the sort of tree you might be able to climb, so you want to get up into the rocks or squeeze into a culvert under the road, if you can run that far. But when Habib once did, a mile from here on a little jeep track, the elephant found where he was and knelt and reached as deeply as she could into the culvert to grab him with her trunk. Then, when that failed, she got up and stood over it and stamped her feet, trying to squash it in on top of him.

We saw a wedding procession, led by a man with a sambar-skin drum and a man with an oboe-length flute. The new couple, returning to town after the ceremony, stopped their approach at the first tea house and were offered free cups of milk by way of welcome. *We* had tea so hot you had to pour it back and forth from cup to saucer (which of course is what you want in a spot where boiling is essential).

That night, a leopard came into somebody's house through an unshuttered window and killed a goat, but was unable to pull it loose from its rope and get it back out the window—so simply crouched, licking its blood at the throat. The owner of the goat, in trying to save it, had been so flustered when the leopard looked at him as if she might pounce that he tripped and broke his arm. But his neighbors, rushing over, frightened the leopard out. This same troublesome female, with kittens to feed, had grabbed a small boy one evening a few weeks before and started to haul him away by his head. But he was quite heavy, slow to drag, and his father bravely gave chase, caught up, and rescued his son, who was all right now, though we saw the tooth marks.

The Irulas had been the indigenous tribe here along the Moyar River—hunters and trackers, snake catchers and soothsayers—and still had a few cohesive villages in the forest. My impression was that they were holding together marginally better than the Todas or Kadars: this partly because they still had a recognized function. Few people in modern India cared whether the surviving Kadars, such as

Sabrimathu, could still track tigers, or whether the few Todas who were left, like M'Thekalmudi, still sang poems to their Temple Buffalo, if they could find her. But the Irulas until very recently had caught cobras for snake charmers all over India—they were the ur-snake charmers—and also as guard figures for traditionalist temples in places where the native cobras had been wiped out. They also caught crocodiles for the World Wildlife Fund's "Crocodile Bank," near Madras, from which Moyar River breeding stock may be reseeded to other zoos or wildlife preserves anywhere crocodiles will be wanted, down the road. Nor are the Irulas' clairvoyant powers to be sneezed at in a country where spiritual telepathy is not confined to mosque, church, or temple. Nonetheless, they, too, were hunkered down in hardscrabble poverty.

We met Murukan, a young Irula man named for an ancient Tamil and Hindu god always seen with a trident. His other name was Bear because, five years earlier, he had been gripped and bitten by a bear—he too has scars—which his father drove off by ripping a handful of thatch from their roof and setting it afire. He said his grandmother was so tough that she once killed a bear with her bare hands that had attacked her when she was coming home from the market on the footpath. His grandfather, a famous hunter who had simply ignored the skein of new wildlife laws that were instituted during his lifetime, called the forestry officer of the Moyar district to his house when he knew he was dying and turned over a whole stack of three hundred skins of animals he had killed with his muzzle-loader over the years— deer and bear for meat, and prowling leopards, or whatever. He had done what was only natural, and not then sold them to smugglers, but wished to be sure his family would not get in trouble. His other gesture, in preparing for death, was to go to their private temple in the woods and remove the statues that mattered to him, such as, Murukan said, a five-foot brass cobra, a silver tiger and a silver bear, a gallon-sized god's head and a sacred ax, and bury them secretly in a pit where not even his descendants would ever discover them, so that they wouldn't suffer the neglect he foresaw for all precious objects and the beliefs undergirding them.

Of course he was right; they would have been stolen. Even the live cobras Murukan still catches to guard the little temple now get killed by passersby who don't realize or accept their significance, and the wider market for temple cobras has dried up. Another Irula family began catching pythons, instead, for a shoe-leather dealer. They got paid the equivalent of five to twenty-five dollars—for a python "large enough to eat a small child"—but started experiencing strange mishaps and very bad luck, and soon stopped.

Murukan's father collects tamarind seeds in the forest for about a dollar per thirty kilos, though it can be dangerous because the elephants collect them also. Other Irulas spend the night on platforms in the paddy fields for a dollar a night, throwing firecrackers or lighting piles of hay to fend off the wild pigs and elephants. (Three years ago, two of them had been stomped on and killed.) Murukan himself—wiry and untidy like a man of the woods—collects honey for a living every March, and had spotted nine beehives on the cliffs so far by a careful reconnaissance. The bees place them as inaccessibly as they can, but he slips on a bedsheet with eyeholes cut in it and works at night, rappelling down the cliff from above, with a burning stick tied to his belt for extra protection and a big tin jar to fill. Each of these hives may provide him with about ten dollars' worth of honey and wax. And there were eleven Irulas, he said, working the ramparts of the cliffs stretching above us, who find two or three hundred hives altogether, though the bears and the leopards diligently compete with them, sometimes almost alongside.

As many as forty British officers used to come to the Moyar River every year to hunt on horseback with tiger hounds; and four Irulas, including Murukan's grandfather, served as trackers, while their wives did the cooking. "The bad tigers but not the good tigers" were killed, and because Irula girls were famously beautiful, some of the bachelor Englishmen would pay a bride price for one of them and carry her off as a mistress to Mysore, Bangalore, or the Malabar Coast. It was not considered too bad a fate, compared to that of the girls who were simply stolen, or seemed to be—eloped or were kidnapped and disappeared. The magical part was that a certain large-ruffed, three-tined sambar deer would come for them and stand on the riverbank, and the next time they went down for water they were never seen again. But when the parents went to the temple to pray, the message conveyed was that their daughter was alive and safe. And what was exasperating was that the Irulas suspected another tribe's magic, the Kurumbas', was operating and surpassing theirs. A Kurumba scout in human form, walking down from his village way up in the Nilgiris for many hours, would have been seen around the Irulas' settlement for a few days, chatting with people, observing everybody. Then he'd leave (and this happened until the 1980s), and the next thing they knew, the sambar materialized on the riverbank again—an apparition they dared not shoot.

The Todas had told me that the first Toda man had found the Buffalo Tree—where buffaloes were given to mankind—

when he happened to be resting underneath it and discovered a horn half-buried in the ground, and became curious as to what the horn was. So I asked Murukan how the Irulas had discovered their own special woods temple, from long before his grandfather's time. It is separate from the several Hindu temples in the valley and the other temples—tiny, prehistoric stone lean-tos that Habib was showing me—whose origins and provenance nobody knew. *Theirs*, the Irulas', was built of mud and grass, over a black stone that, he said, a cow had kept going to, secretly, voluntarily, and dripping her milk upon. When the people who owned her figured out that she was always coming back from the forest with an empty udder, they were angry and followed her, intending to kill whoever was stealing their milk. Instead, they discovered that she was honoring and feeding the black stone. So they built the little mud temple, and, by legend, the stone will crack if any impieties are committed around it. This is where they still bring the skins of chital deer and other creatures that they shoot for food, not selling them but building a hutment with them, praying over them, and later laying others on.

I asked whether Murukan ever encountered a tiger. He said, through Habib's translation, that, yes, four months ago, when he was doing one of his preliminary searches for beehives up a tributary valley—he pointed it out—he had seen a tiger with kittens that "could leap sixty feet" and had just killed a cow. She was crouching over it, sucking blood from its throat and, like a nervy cat, tapping the top of her head with the tuft on the end of her tail. No tiger had killed anybody recently, but five people had been killed by elephants in the past eight years (one man tusked to death in front of our rest house). Yet the elephant is "the king of the jungle," he said, and shouldn't be shot, no matter what he does. During the latest frenzy of poaching, an elephant had been found in the forest here, disabled and kneeling but still alive, with his trunk nailed to the ground with a sharpened crowbar, and L-shaped cuts under his cheeks where his tusks had been cut out. That kind of thing "may be why they're mad."

The Irulas live in an older though now subsidiary hamlet called Hallimoyar, three miles by trail from Thengumarahda. Hallimoyar is named for Queen Halli (plus Moyar), called Hallirani, whose ruined fortress overlooks Thengumarahda from an isolated, heroic-looking spur where she and possibly a thousand men won renown by holding out against the army of Tippu Sultan, the so-called Tiger of Mysore, on one of his predatory raids of the late eighteenth century. The actual village, though, is down in a lovely, well-watered glen in the palm of the valley, under the generous shade of banyan and mango trees, with banana orchards and paddy fields, and even a couple of vacation cottages owned by rich tea planters from the highlands. Thengumarahda is much busier during the daylight hours than Hallimoyar, having many more people—perhaps five hundred. But both shut down at dark, except for the glow of a few oil lamps and a couple of generators, and of course firelight.

The daily routine in Thengumarahda begins at dawn or a little later, when the women get up, bathe, walk several times around a ceremonial minty plant that grows in the houseyard, and do "puja," praying at the family altar. They bring coffee to their husbands and, in old-fashioned households, kneel ritually to him, as according to the adage, "Whether he is grass or a stone, he is still my husband." After sunrise the cattle, which had been closely penned in the middle of the village overnight, have been milked and are moving out of town in one direction. Then when the streets are clear of them, the buffaloes are herded out in another. And flocks of goats follow last—all to graze on the slopes and bottomlands three or four miles out of town.

Men do the herding. The women get the children off to school, and process the surplus milk into ghee, collect and dry the night's dung for fertilizer, carry water to refill their storage containers, gather thorn fencing, or work in small sisterly parties in the fields, alongside a little brigade of men. It is not a money economy (though we met a woman who said she would buy thirty-two kilos of raw rice for the equivalent of seven dollars and convert it to fifty kilos of white rice to sell in her store). But there was abundant food, and to a visitor it seemed sufficiently idyllic that I had to remind myself it was no fun to fear this mother leopard every time she had cubs. Last year she had succeeded in carrying away two babies, and now the men were setting a homemade box trap for her again, with a goat inside. Also, I stopped by the medical clinic on a day that the young student who doctored people was in. With his undergraduate degree, he was studying for his exams to enter medical school, and meanwhile was paid by the government to commute by bus from Satyamangalam to Thengumarahda once a week to give out pills, put on splints, and tell people when they ought to go to a hospital. He said the diseases here were respiratory funguses from the animal dung and TB and asthma; intestinal troubles from the sewage gutters and the stream water; scabies and other skin ailments; and venereal disease from what he called loose morals resulting from the people "having no entertainment," plus the forestry officials bringing germs in and inflicting them on the local girls whom they hired when they were in town.

I was now accompanied by two more travel agents, besides Habib. Mahesh and Danesh were from Madras. Mahesh, the older, more sleek and posh of the two brothers, had just married a Brahman stockbroker's daughter and had plans for the Moyar River valley. He spoke of it as a "product" to "market," and had contracted for half a dozen new skinboats to be built so that his father's big agency could bring in tourists and have them float to or from Thengumarahda. I wasn't enthusiastic about the idea (in fact, have postponed describing this trip for several years in order not to assist the project) and told Danesh, the younger, less socially ambitious, still slightly rebellious brother, that I hoped he'd protect the town as best he could from what might happen if it became a "profit center." He had once saved a village girl from drowning in a well, which was regarded as quite extraordinary: a rich university student from the city risking his life for a peasant girl. And Danesh had another village girl's name tattooed on his shoulder, and said his present girlfriend was not from Madras either, but another region, a lesser social class, and spoke a language he didn't know: so they used English. In the old India, before you could make money writing airline tickets, he said his caste would have been that of a metalworker.

With Danesh and Habib, I went to visit the town blacksmith, a modest, cheery man pounding iron implements over a bellows stove. Then to the brickworks, and the yard where all of Thengumarahda's red roof tiles were made. There was a basket maker, too, and a sizable house filled with silkworm cocoons, a cottage industry that the village had recently started and made a go of. And the town raftsman received a living for poling people and freight across the river in his buffalo-hide skinboat, which, being round and framed with bamboo, could spin in the currents like a carnival ride. The town fisherman, whose name was Kaliappen, netted catfish, carp, and eels to sell and, on the side, guided hydroelectric and forestry surveyors or foreigners such as me.

The town potter was also a sculptor, creating the temple statuary. Like an artist, he acted a bit offish and prickly when Kaliappen took me to see him. Asleep on his verandah at an hour when others weren't, and naked except for a G-string, he was mildly drunk. Humorous, well-knit, fiftyish, and disgruntled when he was told that I might write about him for an American magazine, he departed from type by wanting anonymity. Instead of being pleased and beginning to preen, like your average artistic hustler, he didn't wish for any publicity. He "worked for the gods," he said, through Habib's translation. "What I do is between me and the gods!" Then, as Kaliappen rebuked him for being huffy to a visitor, he softened his manner, told me he hoped that I "lived like a king of kings," and asked politely if I had "walked all the way from America." But he repeated that his name should not be linked with his sculpture, which was an offering to God.

Kaliappen said that we Americans got on an airplane just as if it were a bus. But though a waterman himself—he had a snug skinboat—he'd never seen the ocean. (Nor had Murukan; so the two of them eventually went to Madras on the same train as me, courtesy of Mahesh—who was not too bad a guy—for a first awesome look.) Kaliappen, being a neighbor of the sculptor, then offered us the hospitality of his own verandah, where we sipped coconut water and ate onion and chili rice patties, as the parakeets came screaming back to roost in the coconut palms over us and the sun set.

With Kaliappen as our guide, we drove ten miles upriver the next day in Theena, our 1977 Willys Jeep. Though the riverbank was adorned with a gallery of tropical trees of the most majestic, convoluted proportions, the floor of the valley, unirrigated and under dry ridges, was a veldtlike landscape of scrubby thorn trees, a few foxes and chitals, and no place for a walker to hide if attacked. He showed us where some forestry officials had shot a wild buffalo for a barbecue, and where two years ago an engineer, foolishly on foot while crossing between loops of the river, had been mashed by a mother elephant, who let nobody retrieve his body for the next two days.

We saw five sambars—glorious big deer—and two lithe black bucks—antelopes with spirally horns—all running away; and several quail. The elephants had scoured a red salt lick with their tusks and trunks into the shape of a huge fry pan. It made us glad to spend the night at a cement-block camp by the river that the hydrologists had built, empty now but uncrushable if a herd came through, as tracks showed that they often did. The purling river was seductive, however, with its deep sand beach and noble trees. We tiptoed back and forth repeatedly from the impregnable house to the luscious riverbank, despite hearing that Kaliappen, Mahesh, and Mahesh's father—"the M.D.," they called him, meaning managing director of the travel agency—had been surrounded by elephants and marooned on the riverbank for six hours on the last trip. I was angered when somebody found a harmless trinket snake, an inoffensive species like a garter snake in the U.S., and disabled and dissected it while its heart was still beating. But during the night the stars formed a diamond pattern in the center of the sky and hyenas came sobbing to the fringes of our camp. We slept outside in order to feast upon the sky's beauty, but the price of doing that, of course, was that I dreamt that a hyena was creeping up to devour my foot.

In the morning we got into Kaliappen's coracle, the prototype of what the tourists would ride, and pushed off. The flow was brisk, the current a clean earthy brown. Skimming along as probably the first rafters in months, we saw a plenitude of creatures that had come to the Moyar to drink, or lived anyway under the drapery of trees. Brown catlike monkeys and midsized swinging langurs, peacocks and jungle fowl, black bucks and chital deer, and several sambars that spooked when they saw us. Eight wild buffaloes that had been wading in the water also ran. An eagle watched us from a limb, and several vultures were circling a kill that was up on the bank, out of view. A blackish crocodile slid off the beach and others, swimming, slowly dived. There were Malabar squirrels, one lying dead, apparently of a snakebite, and parrots, bulbuls, hoopoes, bee-catchers, hornbills, and a fish owl moaning *boom-oh-boom*.

"Don't you want other Americans to see this?" Habib asked me.

"But they won't," I suggested. "Everything will drink at night."

Kaliappen said that the monkeys had already fled from us so precipitously because their blood is sometimes drunk as a tonic for asthma—just as bear meat is chewed small and fed to infants to make them grow strong, and tiger dung is rubbed on skin ailments, and ground-up bits of elephants' teeth are swallowed for internal aches.

Drifting swiftly on, paddling to avoid an occasional patch of rocks, we found that buffalo hide was a wonderfully resilient covering for a boat if you hit, and roundness an ideal shape for collisions because you just spun around and rolled off. I told them that much of America had been explored by fur trappers in skinboats.

We passed a tree house where hydroelectric technicians sometimes lived while measuring the river's volume and pace. With their ladder, they were safe from the elephants, but otherwise the trees were really too big for them to have climbed.

Floating around a few more bends, we noticed an unusual-looking rock in the shallows by the left shore. It was longer, wider, and higher than most. Kaliappen suddenly muttered, "That's a dead elephant!"

This was a find—sad, mysterious, curious, lucky. But as we approached, dipping our paddles to slow our progress and steer close but not too close, our voices rose and the rock moved. It scrambled to get its feet under it and upright, while we paddled like mad to the opposite bank, jumped out of the skinboat as quick as we could, and clambered up out of sight of the now very lively elephant, which had merely been bathing. We found ourselves in a fallow field with no cover to hide in from the behemoth if it followed us; then scattered at a crouch so it would have to pick only one in particular to chase. Kaliappen yelled at me to take off my white shirt so I wouldn't stick out. But my skin was still pale. Scrunching down, I tried to become earth-color.

After we had waited awhile and determined that the elephant had left without even smashing our skinboat (as had happened to Kaliappen's last), we discovered that we had landed under Hallirani's lofty fortress on its remarkable crag. The field was strewn with random ruins, such as a five-foot temple built of three stone slabs, with another slab laid on top, very ancient, though some contemporary coins had been inserted in the back wall as an offering. The figures of a woman and a lion were discernibly carved in it; and two-foot-high stone hovels of a similar construction stood nearby, that you could have crawled into. Other carved stones lay about in the grass; also an urn for grinding rice, blackened with age and too heavy to lift. I hadn't enough energy to climb to Hallirani's unconquered high-up redoubt, but Habib said that the huge rainwater cistern that had enabled her to withstand Tippu Sultan's siege was still intact—you could take a dip in it—and several links of the thick iron chain that had held the gate, and much of the brick wall that had plugged the gaps between the natural ramparts of rock. And he'd even found a goodly portion of her wooden palanquin, he said. He was trying to interest a university or the government in investigating or salvaging what was left.

When we got back to Thengumarahda, we heard that two cobras had been tussling in a breeding ritual across the little stream from our rest house. An elephant cow and calf had eaten two banana trees when the watchmen fell asleep; and that mother leopard had slipped into town yet again, slid inside somebody's house, grabbed another goat, and gotten away with it.

We talked to a seventy-year-old man who was cultivating a mulberry field. He'd bought a goat for five hundred rupees, nearly a month's pay, he said, and had tethered her next to him as he worked, so she could browse and still be safe. But within a month this same leopard had crept up in the heat of the day, pounced over his stooping back, and seized her, thrown her over *her* back, and carried her up to the spiry knoll where she had her two kittens—kind of a miniature of

Hallirani's refuge, I suggested. He laughed, pointing out just where to climb if I wanted to try bearding her at the mouth of her cave. The queen had lived "at the time when the gods lived here," he told me in Tamil, through Habib's translation.

He showed me a thicket where a bear and her cub had slept last night. Monkeys were whooping in the trees, and he said he'd rather "dig bulbs in the forest" than kill animals for food. His settlement of a dozen families was called Pudha Kadu, "New Place," and had its own little whitewashed mud, dung, and stone temple, a single room with a head-high thatched roof. One of my sculptor friend's terra-cotta elephants stood at the entrance, facing a black rock that had been chosen from the Moyar's riverbed after much deliberation by a young boy "who had god in him," the old man said. Inside were five other river stones that had been similarly identified by this inspired boy. Each was painted with eyes and a turmeric forehead dot. Six brass plates leaning on a shelf depicted a female deity named Masiniyathi, and there were several holy elephants, and a vessel holding coconut water that people sprinkled on themselves, and two china plates containing a sacred ash to dab on one's forehead. Three paintings showed the god Murukan with his trident, riding a peacock; and jolly Ganesha with his sidekick, the rat; and their joined male-and-female parent, Siva and Parvati. Women couldn't enter the temple. Men had to bring the ash and coconut water out to them.

Our Murukan was less used to Europeans, less sophisticated than Kaliappen, and conscientiously poured out my jug of boiled drinking water in order to refill it from the tap because the tapwater looked clearer to him. Though Kaliappen loved wild things and was an enthusiastic observer— instinctively a conservationist—he wasn't twinned with them like Murukan. Agile, stocky Kaliappen had once "ridden" a wild buffalo to distract it from trampling a friend who'd been knocked to the ground—had also "ridden" a black buck that he'd caught sleeping, for fun. But Murukan, like Sabrimathu, had a willowy, weavier quality, as spontaneous as the boughs that bounce in the wind, versus a "civilized" superstructure of iron.

We went to see the headman of Murukan's Irula village of Hallimoyar. His name was Siddan and he lived in a one-room concrete house decorated with plastic mango leaves and yellow flowers hanging over the open doorway. A Rotary Club had just paid four hundred rupees to have his cataracts removed at the regional hospital, so he had perhaps more reason than usual to be cheerful. However, the dispiritedness of old age and shattered traditions still seemed to underlie his mood. The government did provide the children of registered tribal people with free schooling, uniforms, and so forth, but he missed the British. He had worked on a coffee plantation six miles uphill, and "We lived like kings," he said in English. "Nobody was hungry." At least not tribal hunters in this Shangri-la, with forest skills. He told me that a cow giving ten liters of milk a day would cost him five thousand rupees, and a buffalo giving half that much, three thousand (or about one hundred dollars). You could borrow up to two thousand rupees from the government, but you'd have to give half back to the authorizing officials as a bribe, plus interest on the whole. Wages were a dollar a day.

A forest fire was burning in a hanging valley; we watched the smoke. But at our rest house I was surprised to see the forestry officers lounging on the porch, watching it so casually. They said they'd "book" somebody for starting it, some hapless shepherd who might have had a campfire, though it was out of the question that they would actually climb up to the fire to try to put it out. A sandalwood smuggler might have been the culprit, Siddan said, or merely the prism of a broken bottle left there years ago, and not the nearest shepherd at all.

Next day, a holy man, a sadhu, hiked into Thengumarahda. Tall, thirty-something, with uncut hair and wearing an orange turban and orange shorts, he was sitting on a stone wall along the wagon path, nodding to people he knew. His air of exuberance also made him stand out. As it happened, this was his hometown. He had a wife and four children here, he told me with Habib's help, but a year or so ago he had had a vision from God. He had talked with God, and with his wife's acquiescence "because it was from God," he had left home to wander the world. His face looked buoyant, and besides his scanty orange clothing, he wore multiple strings of brown beads and had painted red and white tridents on his forehead and bare chest and arms. He carried only a plastic bag such as animal feed is sold in, into which the villagers on his travels could pour donations of rice, to keep him going, or where he put the cannabis plants that Habib said he probably picked wild. Inside the plastic bag was a pretty pouch made from a chital deer's red-and-white spotted skin. Inside this special pouch—as he showed me when I asked—he had a plate-sized brass gong that he struck, and a conch shell that he blew, before he said his prayers.

According to Habib, freelance sadhus like him sometimes fulfilled a role similar to that of psychotherapists in the West. They talked and listened to families whose temple priest might seem consumed with performing the daily rituals, or otherwise oblique, opaque, and obtuse. Many hamlets had no priest, and sadhus, by their lectures and by stimulating acts of charity beyond their own needs, offered visible testimony to consecrated traditions that otherwise could have lapsed. They also revisited abandoned shrines, forgotten temples, and other precious sites in their impromptu roamings, under the ancient rubric that improvisation can engender inspiration. And by trusting themselves not just to humanity but to the wilderness, they were generally able to pass by elephants and tigers without being molested.

Seeing my interest was sincere, this sadhu told me I could go with him tomorrow to a temple in a valley an eight-hour walk away that "belonged to the animals." That is, the valley did; but as a consequence the temple still had its silver statues. Once, a man from Thengumarahda had walked all that way to steal them, but fell so sick a week later he had to walk all the way back and return them.

Kaliappen ended up taking Habib, Danesh, and me on a stroll that was nearly as challenging. We went on a picnic to catch some fish and look at crocodile drag-marks in the sand on a plump beach three miles below Hallimoyar. The river rustled by in corded currents under grandly proportioned trees. We built a driftwood fire for cooking, and napped when we weren't doing anything else. An elephant path crossed the Moyar at this point, and we found hyena prints and dung with sambar hair in it. You could wade out in the silky water and sit on a knobby rock, or cradle yourself on the lowest limbs of two or three of the biggest trees that arced over the river.

Though it ran hip-deep near the bank, and though a cow was reported to have been bitten on the nose upstream the day before, we trusted Kaliappen's assurance that he knew the nature of crocodiles and enjoyed the afternoon till sunset: whereupon we started walking back to Hallimoyar on the ox-wagon track. A brown-and-white Brahminy kite was being buzzed by a swift gray hawk. We'd seen a black buck, fleeing us in a hurry, on our trip in, and expected to stumble upon other animals as dusk approached. A river temple stood along the trail with a cobra living in a termite mound alongside that Murukan had said he'd put there. A rich tea planter from the heights had paid to have the site spruced up. It was an open-sided platform with pillars supporting the roof and lions on top of that, as well as other stone or terra-cotta statuary brought from afar, not merely the sort of mud figures that people made for themselves to save money and then painted white, as often is the case. But the situation was genuinely antique, rediscovered in historic times (Murukan had told me) by a shepherd who used to lie under a certain shady tree here, as his cattle nibbled through the woods—but felt uncannily itchy when he did. His curiosity had been so aroused that he dug with his knife and finally unearthed a clay figurine which, when he cut into it, bled.

Though I'd hoped to see the cobra—and there was also a trench for fire walking—we weren't inclined to linger because we'd already waited too long, while dawdling at the beach. It was growing dark. The twelve hours of night would belong to the animals; and as Kaliappen reminded us, five years ago a husband and wife from Thengumarahda who were praying at this temple had been knelt on by an elephant. Furthermore, we smelled carrion. In a comfy Land Rover in East Africa a tourist will follow vultures, but on foot in India at nightfall, we didn't want to know what animal had killed the carcass whose odor was pungently wafting to us.

Clouds hid the moon. We distanced ourselves from whatever might be guarding the meat. Fortunately the path was composed of a whitish soil that we could fix our eyes on. But then I happened to glance up, from telepathy perhaps, and dimly noticed that we were all about to collide with a baby elephant. How nice, I thought for just a second, a baby elephant. *A Baby Elephant!* Then, sure enough, the mother's shape loomed indistinctly in the gloom, five yards away. Her shadowy trunk hardly moved, not yet swinging forward and up; her tree-trunk legs looked the very pattern of patience. But as we alerted one another agitatedly in whispers, her great ears did spread out above us like a cobra's hood. We could also make out other females at her shoulders—two, three waiting, maybe four.

"We're totally trapped. Our luck has gone all bad," whispered Kaliappen.

The elephants were preparing to enter the road, so we didn't run backward. Instead we ran upward, up the side of a rocky ridge that fortuitously stood to our right. They could have charged uphill, but rocks are not to a pachyderm's liking. The steeper and more bouldery it was, the better for us. We scattered, but angled slantwise along the slope to a drop-off that seemed high enough that their trunks couldn't reach us if they followed and stood on their hind legs. Collecting there, we agreed it was the best we could do. Looking down two hundred feet at the trail in a slice of moonlight, we saw more elephants in the dusk. Another group was arriving. We tried to count; thirty or forty were slowly shuffling toward the river. It was amazing, almost surreal in the dark. Fearfully, we lit a fire on a flat part of the rock—and heard a groan from some of the matriarchs below, as though they were murmuring, *What are these crazies gonna do, set the valley, too, on fire?*

After the assemblage apparently had vanished toward the river, we yelled for a couple of hours before a gust of wind caught our voices properly and carried them to the night watchmen in Hallimoyar's paddy fields. Bravely, they set out to rescue us, though in fact they didn't know who we were, and thought we might be bandits, smugglers, poachers, or whatever, seeing our fire. They said later that they had been as scared of us as of the possibility that elephants might be blocking the road. The fire would have protected us for the rest of the night from cats, bears, bison, dholes, or hyenas, but we were impatient and glad of their cooperative spirit.

Back at Thengumarahda, a troupe of actors of the Koothu Theater in Madras was performing the great Hindu seventh-century epic cycle of the Mahabharata for the villagers. The show, in bravura style, lasted for eight hours through the night, and though not puppetry, reminded me of the classic Sicilian puppet shows that dramatize in marvelous fashion the epics of Charlemagne.

Swiftly, the next day, we left by oxcart, skinboat, and soon our Willys Jeep again. Back to the mad, pool-table traffic of India, with me hallucinating accidents from the death seat that never quite occurred. The rickety horse wagon piled with sugarcane and the lorry overloaded with gravel converging just ahead of us on the skinny, skinny road—surely we couldn't squeeze through? But maybe precisely because we were traveling at sixty and shimmying, we would do so. To have slowed, or steered less reflexively, might have meant a smashup.

In Coimbatore, the "Pest Man," the "Auto Consultancy," the "Polio Clinic," the "Bone-Setting Hospital," "Guru Travels," and cracker shops, tool shops, pickle shops, flower shops, diamond shops, peddlers selling watermelons, mustard seed, tomatoes, people plaiting palm leaves for roof thatch, spinning coconut fiber into ropes. A red-headed devil's effigy hung from a beam in a building being constructed, to forestall accidents. On several doors three stripes were drawn with ashes, top and bottom, mourning a death. And in the morning in many neighborhoods, women in saris stooped to draw complex, improvised, geometrical but wavy designs with rice powder on the sidewalk in front of their doors, which mutely but sometimes quite powerfully broadcast the state of harmony or else dissonance in their households—the daily mood engendered by the kind of spouse and children they had. (It's supposed to be rice powder so that the ants may eat, too.)

In Madras, "Eve-teasers"—bumptious men who torment women in public places—shared the clattering streets with beige and yellow sacred cows, which roamed free, willfully, impulsively, though always glad to find a banana skin or an orange rind, and were milked and fed grass by the very poor. Bullocks, on the other hand, labored with a rope strung through their septums. We have won the earth from other vertebrates by our exceptional lubricity; and foreplay remains the basis of most commercial advertising, as billboards everywhere make plain. But people in India rock their heads agreeably, as they talk to each other, to show sociability, which to a Westerner is confusing because the motion looks instead like a minute form of head shaking, as if they're disagreeing.

My plane's departure from Madras was delayed because
in New Delhi there were bomb scares at the airport. Busi-
nessmen were leaving the capital with their families before
the religious riots that were scheduled for tomorrow. So,
feeling in suspension, I persuaded a guy at the terminal to
drive me up a nearby hill where Doubting Thomas (according to some reports) was crucified. It seems natural that, in
his regret or sense of guilt for having at first doubted Christ's
resurrection, Saint Thomas would have been the apostle
who proselytized the furthest afterwards—clear to the Bay
of Bengal, perhaps, here to recapitulate Christ's fate. I've felt
a link to Thomas because my parents used to call me "Doubting Thomas" when I was young and rebellious and "doubted"
their Episcopalian liturgy. Maybe among his minor com-
plaints at the last was a bellyache just like mine from eating
curried rice and vegetable patties on a banana leaf.

Yet on this cathedral hill, schoolchildren were planting
trees, while a gang of jackdaws disputed possession of the
sky with some vultures and kites, and the smell of uric acid
and rotting carbohydrates drifted up from Madras's five million people below. But I also saw an egret sitting on a cow's
back, and a blackbird on a buffalo. Cashew trees, brick
kilns, papaya trees, droves of white ducks on the way to
market, and even a drove of pigs. The Cooum River divides
the city.

Brahma, Vishnu, and Siva—Creator, Preserver, and
Destroyer—riding, respectively, on a Swan, an Eagle and a
Bull, had topped Saint Thomas's appeal in India. More din,
more heterogeneity, plus the androgynous exuberance of so
many sculpted figures from the animal kingdom scrambling
like totems up the compact temple towers. Metaphors, of

course, but with a bit of glee or mischief thrown in, and the undergirding of real elephants, cobras, lions (yes, lions lived in India), and tigers maybe only a day's walk away.

One does not leave wild places hopefully now. Alloys indeed are what we'll have. Virtual wildernesses and realities; metafictions. "Albino king snakes" are already in the pet stores, and "ligers" and "tiglons" in the dealers' catalogs that hobbyists use. (Apparently, selling a cross evades the endangered species laws.) But I exaggerate. Winnie the Pooh was an alloy of a kind, and the rear-guard actions for preservation many people are fighting will stave off curtain time for a while.

When I remember that Siberian tiger caged in eighteen square feet in the circus, or the black-maned but supernumerary movie lion I cared for in California in 1953—who had been relegated to a reinforced piano box—I can't romanticize how such things were fifty years ago. The cruelty was abominable, but was still encysted in a world that seemed closer to being whole. Ultimate wild things are incidentally dangerous—white sharks, gorgeous tigers, harpy eagles, polar bears—as well as unpredictable. Tigers are less athletic, more complicated, than a leopard, which may sometimes seem like a single, lengthy muscle. A tiger's spirit, when ferocious, feline, and imperial, can parallel ours, though without the monkeying primate qualities that have given us our berserk streak that invents the end of the world. Tigers are less heartbreaking than the beleaguered elephant because they are not social creatures and are reactive, not innovative. But they are an apex, a kind of hook the web of nature hangs on. To know them, and elephants, marked my life.